COLLINS
COBUILD

ENGLISH GUIDES
7: METAPHOR

WITHDRAWN FROM STOCK

Alice Deignan

D1439636

THE UNIVERSITY
OF BIRMINGHAM

COLLINS
COBUILD

HarperCollins*Publishers*

425 /1480756

HarperCollins Publishers
77-85 Fulham Palace Road
London W6 8JB

COBUILD is a trademark of William Collins Sons & Co Ltd

© HarperCollins Publishers Ltd 1995
First published 1995
Reprinted 1997

10 9 8 7 6 5 4 3 2

All rights reserved. No part of this book may be reproduced, stored
in a retrieval system, or transmitted in any form or by any means,
electronic, mechanical, photocopying, recording or otherwise,
without the prior permission in writing of the Publisher.

ISBN 0 00 370952 3

Computer typeset by Tradespools Ltd, Frome, Somerset

Printed in Great Britain by Caledonian International Book
Manufacturing Ltd, Glasgow, G64

For Robert and Elizabeth Roe

Corpus Acknowledgements

We would like to acknowledge the assistance of the many hundreds
of individuals and companies who have kindly given permission for
copyright material to be used in The Bank of English. The written
sources include many national and regional newspapers in Britain and
overseas; magazine and periodical publishers; and book publishers in
Britain, the United States, and Australia. Extensive spoken data has
been provided by radio and television broadcasting companies; research
workers at many universities and other institutions; and numerous
individual contributors. We are grateful to them all.

The COBUILD Series

Founding Editor-in-Chief   John Sinclair

Editorial Team

Editorial Director   Gwyneth Fox

Series Editor   Jane Bradbury

Computer Staff   Tim Lane
Andrea Lewis

Secretarial Staff   Sue Crawley
Michelle Devereux

HarperCollins *Publishers*
Gillian McNair

Acknowledgements

The author would also like to thank: Annette Capel; Alex Collier;
Professor Malcolm Coulthard; Tim Deignan; Dr Susan Hunston;
Ramesh Krishnamurthy; Elizabeth Manning; Dr Rosamund Moon;
Christina Rammell.

Contents

Introduction

The Use of Metaphors in Current English

Many words have both literal and metaphorical meanings. The literal meaning of a word is its most basic sense. A metaphorical meaning is when it is used to refer to something other than this.

Thousands of words are used metaphorically in English, not just in literary or poetic language, but in everyday language such as journalism and conversation. For example, the literal meaning of **root** is a part of a plant. **Root** is used metaphorically to refer to the cause of a situation, especially a situation that is a problem. It is interesting to note that the metaphorical uses of some words, such as **root**, **drive**, and **build**, are so common that most native speakers no longer think of the literal meaning of the word when they are using them metaphorically.

The study of metaphor has traditionally been associated with the study of literature, but, as Lakoff and Johnson pointed out in their important book, *Metaphors We Live By*, (Chicago University Press, 1980), the use of metaphor is not restricted to this kind of language. A good understanding of how metaphor is used in everyday language is important for students of English, not only so that they can increase their vocabulary, but also so that they can understand new or original metaphors when they hear or read them. Most languages make use of metaphor, but the way individual words are used varies from one language to another, and so it is important that students are aware that each language has its own system, and that they cannot always transfer the metaphorical use of a word from one language to another.

How To Use This Guide

This Guide is arranged in twelve chapters, each of which deals with a particular theme, such as **plants**, **health and illness**, or **sport and games**, looking at how words whose literal meanings are associated with these subjects are used metaphorically.

By explaining the link between the literal and the metaphorical uses of the word, and giving plenty of real examples of how they are used, this Guide encourages students to develop a deeper understanding of how metaphor is really used in current English.

Teachers can use each of the chapters as the basis for classroom discussions and exercises, for example, by asking students to look at a passage of text and identify the metaphors used in it, and then encouraging them to discuss how this compares with the way words are used in their own first language.

The Bank of English

This book, like all COBUILD books, is derived from studying the evidence in the Bank of English, which contains over 200 million words. The examples are taken directly from the corpus and the frequency of words affects the prominence given to them here. By using the Bank of English we were also able to discover which words occur most frequently with each metaphor. This is shown in the explanation of the metaphor and in the examples. Where it is useful, a list of words which occur frequently with a particular metaphor is given.

So many words are used metaphorically in English that it would not be possible for a book this size to cover them all. Instead, this book focuses on some of the most common ones. When you are looking at a particular chapter, you might like to think of whether you have come across other words with similar meanings being used metaphorically.

You might also like to try to think of other groups of words that are used metaphorically, such as words associated with water, clothes, or cleaning.

We hope that you find this book helpful and easy to use. Please write to us with any comments or suggestions about how to improve COBUILD publications. We have set up an e-mail address (editors@cobuild.collins.co.uk) to make it easier for users to correspond with us. You can write to us at the following address:

COBUILD
Instutute of Research and Development
University of Birmingham Research Park
Vincent Drive
Birmingham B15 2SQ

1 The Human Body

1.1 Many words which refer to parts of the body are used metaphorically. This chapter looks at some of the most common of these beginning with the word **body** itself, then moving on to the **head** and **face**, including the **eyes**, **ears**, **nose**, and **lips**. Next, various other parts of the body are discussed, such as **the skeleton**, **the spine**, **backbone**, **shoulder**, **hand**, **blood**, and **guts**, and finally two verbs which refer to processes your body performs; **swallow** and **digest**.

The body

1.2 Your **body** is all your physical parts, including your head, arms, legs, and all your internal organs. This idea of a collection of separate parts working together is used metaphorically to refer to groups or organizations made up of separate parts which work together to perform a particular task.

1.3 A particular **body** is a group of people who have been officially organized in order to deal with a particular situation or problem.

He has set up a body called the Security Council.
...a framework for these new political, administrative and legal bodies.
...the world governing body in athletics.

1.4 You can refer to a group of people who share feelings and beliefs and who work towards a common aim as a particular **body**.

Although he is only 31, he has a growing body of followers.

1.5 A **body of** information or knowledge is a large amount of information or knowledge, usually on a particular subject, which has been gathered together in an organized way so that people can study it or refer to it.

Various statistical publications were used to supplement the main body of information.
There certainly is a large body of evidence to support these notions.

The head

1.6 Your **head** is the part of your body that contains your brain, and important sense organs such as your eyes, ears, and nose. It is the processes that take place in these organs that control how your body works and how you think and feel, and so **head** is used metaphorically to refer to the person who is in charge of or responsible for a particular group or organization. For example, the **head** of a government is the leader of that government.

He had also worked for a time in business in Paris and as head of modern languages at a London grammar school.
The tour is the first visit to the country by a Jewish head of state.
...international meetings with heads of state and UN representatives.

1.7 **Head** is also used as a verb with this meaning. If someone **heads** a group or organization, they are in charge of it and are responsible for its actions.

He will head a provisional government.
He heads a group representing the families of the British victims.

The face

1.8 The word **face** and words for parts of the face such as **eye** and **nose** are used metaphorically to refer to particular atttitudes, emotions, or ways of behaving.

face

1.9 Your **face** is the part of you that shows your expressions, such as a smile if you are happy or a frown if you are worried. Your expressions reveal to other people how you are feeling and so, if you do not want people to know how you feel about something, you can try to alter or control the expressions on your face. **Face** is used metaphorically to refer to the way people and organizations present themselves to others.

People sometimes refer to the public image of a person or organization as a particular **face** of that person or organization, especially when they want to suggest that there are other, very different aspects of that person or organization.

...the acceptable face of Soviet foreign policy.
He may have difficulty persuading the security forces to adopt a more human face.

1.10 If someone **loses face**, they are embarrassed publicly, and feel upset and humiliated as a result of this. If someone **saves face**, they manage to avoid being embarrassed publicly, or if they have been embarrassed publicly, they do something to make the situation better.

You should never be made to feel that you have lost face.
They run away from the problem, hoping it will disappear of its own accord, lying to save face.

1.11 If someone **puts on a brave face**, or **puts a brave face on** a bad situation, they try to behave in public as if they were not upset or unhappy about their problems or failures.

Patrick tried to <u>put on a brave face</u> but he was terribly worried.
He did his best to <u>put a brave face on</u> his failure.

In American English, the expression **put on a good face** is also used.

Scientists are <u>putting a good face on</u> their troubles.

1.12 If you **face** someone **down**, you oppose or confront them and defeat them by appearing very confident and brave, even if you do not really feel very confident or brave.

He's confronted crowds before and <u>faced</u> them <u>down</u>.
He'd spent a lifetime <u>facing down</u> lesser men, men who lacked his courage.

1.13 If you **face** the truth, a fact, or a problem, or if you **face up to it**, you accept it and begin to deal with it, even though you do not really want to do so. If you **face** someone with the truth, a fact, or a problem, you try to make them accept that it is true or that it really exists.

Although your heart is breaking, you must <u>face</u> the truth that the relationship is ended.
He accused the government of refusing to <u>face</u> facts about the economy.
They were having to <u>face up to</u> the fact that they had lost everything.

1.14 If you **cannot face** a problem or a situation, you feel as if you cannot deal with it because it seems so unpleasant, difficult, or frightening.

I <u>couldn't face</u> the prospect of spending a Saturday night there.
I <u>couldn't face</u> seeing anyone.

eye

1.15 You use your **eyes** to look at and judge real objects in the world around you. Because of this, the **eyes** are associated with the way you judge situations and behaviour, and the attitude you have towards them.

1.16 If you see an event or situation **through** someone else's **eyes**, you understand it in the way that that person would understand it.

She would never look at snow <u>through</u> the <u>eyes</u> of a child again.
You see London <u>through</u> the <u>eyes</u> of a tourist and do things you wouldn't normally do.

I tried for a moment to see the situation through her eyes.

1.17 If you say that something is the case **in** a particular person's **eyes**, or **in the eyes of** a particular person, you mean that this is the way they judge it or consider it, although other people may judge it or consider it in a different way.

In his eyes, I'm still a student.
Even if the parents do split up, they can remain, at least in the eyes of the children, still friends.
In the eyes of the law that is an unforgivable crime.

1.18 If you do one thing **with an eye to** something or someone else, you consider the second person or thing when you do the first thing. If you do one thing **with an eye to** doing another thing, you do the first thing with the intention of doing the second thing as a result of it.

The selections have been made with an eye to the casual buyer.
Much First World aid is provided with at least half an eye to the donor's interest.
The Foreign Office says it's agreed to pay it, but with an eye to claiming the money back at a later date.
Members may join in any of these trips which are usually arranged with an eye to purchasing the best possible travel arrangements at the lowest possible cost.

1.19 If you have **an eye for** certain things, you are good at valuing or judging them because you have experience and knowledge about them.

Developing an eye for a horse is not something which can be taught via a book.
...writing with a sense of local colour and an eye for illuminating detail.

1.20 If someone is **in the public eye**, they are receiving a lot of public attention, for example in the newspapers or on television.

It was not until his retirement that he began the work which has kept his name in the public eye ever since.
A spokesman said: 'When anyone in the public eye is seen smoking it can do nothing but harm.'

1.21 **Eye** can also be used to refer to a part of a physical object which looks like an eye. For example, the hole at one end of a needle is referred to as the **eye** of a needle; dark spots on a potato from which new stems grow are referred to as **eyes**.

nose

1.22 You use your **nose** to smell things. Some animals have a very highly developed sense of smell, and are able to use this sense in very important ways, such as to find food or to sense when danger is near. When it is used metaphorically, **nose** is associated with instinct, especially when it is connected with discovering things or finding things out.

1.23 If you **have a nose for** something, you are able to find or discover it easily, by using your instincts rather than your intelligence or observation.

> He _had a nose for_ a situation. If there was something amiss, he sensed it.
> He _had a nose for_ trouble and a brilliant tactical mind.

1.24 **Nose** is also used to refer to the front section of vehicles such as aircraft and cars.

teeth

1.25 Animals such as dogs, wolves, lions, and tigers have large, strong **teeth** which they use to hunt other animals for foods and when they are fighting to defend themselves or their young. **Teeth** is used metaphorically to talk about strength, power, and aggression.

1.26 If an organization **has teeth**, it is strong, powerful, and aggressive, and is likely to be successful because of this. If it **has no teeth**, it is not strong or powerful enough, and therefore is not likely to be successful. You can also say that something such as a rule or a plan **has teeth** if you want to suggest that it is likely to be successful, especially when you want to suggest that it will be enforced in a powerful or aggressive way. These uses are most common in journalism.

> The resolution will be supported by as many countries as possible and _will have teeth_.
> Since a big part of every employee's compensation is tied to achieving the standards, the system _has teeth_.
> But other instructions to politicians _have had no teeth_. There've been daily violations of a code of conduct which tells politicians to refrain from personal attacks.

Note that the singular form **tooth** is not used in this way.

tongue

1.27 You use your **tongue** to talk, and you can describe the way that someone speaks by saying that they have a particular kind of **tongue**. **Tongue** is often used in this way to say hurtful or negative things about someone.

> She has an acid _tongue_, she can raise laughs at other people's expense.
> He was also by nature an intellectual bully with a cutting _tongue_.

...her quick temper and fierce <u>tongue</u>.

1.28 You can refer to a particular language as a particular **tongue**. **Tongue** is used in this way in written English, especially in novels and journalism.

The Dutch were top with nearly 80% able to chat in a foreign <u>tongue</u>.
Latin was for hundreds of years the common <u>tongue</u> to much of Europe.

1.29 Tongue can also be used to refer to things which are long and thin, like a tongue. For example, a piece of land which stretches out into the sea can be referred to as a **tongue** of land; a single flame can be referred to as a **tongue** of flame.

lip

1.30 Like your tongue, your **lips** are associated with talking and speech. You can refer to disrespectful and rude remarks that someone makes as **lip**. This is an informal use.

That's enough of your <u>lip</u>, Sharon.

Note that the plural form **lips** is not used in this way.

ear

1.31 You use your **ears** to listen to the sounds around you, such as speech and music. **Ear** is used metaphorically to refer to how good someone is at understanding or judging particular things that they hear.

If you have an **ear**, or have a **good ear** for the sounds of something such as music, a language, or ways of speaking, you are very sensitive to them and can interpret or reproduce them well.

He has always had a <u>good ear</u> for a tune.
I'm proud of my extraordinarily <u>good ear</u> for accents and dialects.
He is a good novelist too, with a superb <u>ear</u> for dialogue.

Other parts of the body

shoulder

1.32 When people carry or pull heavy weights, they often use their **shoulders** to support most of the weight. In English, problems are often referred to as burdens, and responsibilities are often said to be heavy or to have weight, and so people are often said to carry problems or responsibilities **on** their **shoulders**.

> *She's an old, wise woman with a lot of responsibility resting on her shoulders.*
> *The government's reforms place too great a burden on the shoulders of the ordinary people.*
> *The fate of the family, it seemed, rested on my shoulders.*
> *The hopes of the nation are on his shoulders.*

Note that the singular form **shoulder** is not used in this way.

1.33 Shoulder is also used as a verb. If you **shoulder** responsibilities, you accept them and take charge of them.

> *His grandfather shouldered the burden of leadership.*
> *The airlines are being asked to shoulder a disproportionate share of the tax.*

heart

1.34 Your **heart** is the organ responsible for making sure that blood is supplied to every part of your body. If your heart stopped working properly, you would become ill and possibly die. Because of this, people often refer to something that they consider to be the most important and influential part of a particular system or organization as the **heart** of it.

> *...Wall Street, the business and financial heart of the United States.*
> *...at the very heart of our culture.*
> *...at the heart of the mystery.*
> *At its heart the issue is not a scientific debate.*

1.35 Your heart is situated in your chest, almost in the centre of your body. People sometimes refer to the part of a place that they consider to be the most central as **the heart of** that place, especially if they want to suggest that it is a very important or busy area.

> *...a three-star hotel in the heart of the Latin quarter.*
> *The restaurant is located in the heart of busy Manchester.*

1.36 People talk about the **heart** as the place where their deepest feelings come from. This is because in former times it was believed that your heart controlled your emotions, especially emotions such as love. These days, **heart** is still used to talk about positive feelings such as love, courage, and happiness. It is often used in expressions which involve words such as **break** which show that something has stopped you from having these positive feelings.

1.37 Heart can be used with adjectives to talk about someone's character and their attitude to other people. For example, if you say that someone has a **warm heart**, you mean that they are kind and generous; if you say that someone has a **cruel heart**, you mean that they are extremely unpleasant to other people and do not seem to care whether or not they suffer.

She loved his brilliance and his generous heart.
She's got a good heart.

1.38 If someone **breaks** your **heart**, they make you feel very sad and unhappy, usually because they end a love affair or close relationship with you.

You broke my heart, Margaret, you wrecked my life.

1.39 If a bad situation or sad event **breaks** your **heart**, it makes you feel extremely unhappy or disappointed.

It broke her heart to see him go.
...living in a state of filth and disease that would break your heart.
He hasn't been to see our two young sons for a couple of months and it's breaking their hearts.

1.40 If someone is **heart-broken,** they are very unhappy.

If anything happened to the baby you would be heart-broken.
There had been a row with her boyfriend, and she was heart-broken.

1.41 If you describe an event or situation as **heart-breaking,** you mean that it makes you feel very sad.

The team that refused to be beaten on so many occasions finally had to accept the bitter, heart-breaking reality of failure.
Her letters have been heart-breaking.

1.42 If your **heart goes out to** someone, you sympathize very deeply with their problems.

My heart goes out to this compassionate man. How could anyone see him as a criminal?
Her sincerity and her unhappiness were clear and his heart went out to her.

1.43 If someone has a **change of heart**, their feelings towards something change. If a government or large organization has a **change of heart**, their policy towards something changes.

What has brought about this sudden change of heart?
Has the National Party had a change of heart, and if so, why?

This is a massive change of heart by the German central bank which only recently put up German rates by 0.75%.

1.44 If you feel or know something **in** your **heart**, you feel or believe it very strongly, but you may not want to talk about or accept this feeling or knowledge.

She knew in her heart that one day she would have to leave him.
Deep in his heart he believed that he could persuade her if he only asked often enough.
I just couldn't bring myself to admit what I knew in my heart was true.

1.45 There are several expressions using **heart** which refer to courage and determination.

1.46 If you **take heart**, you become more courageous. If you **lose heart**, you feel discouraged and lose the determination to continue what you were doing.

Take heart, for all is not lost.
Until now he had managed to keep up his classes at the University, but he lost heart for study and dropped out of school.

1.47 If your **heart sinks**, or if you feel a **sinking** of your **heart**, something which you hear or see makes you feel very discouraged and depressed.

There was no sign of him, and her heart sank.
I felt a definite sinking of the heart.

1.48 Something that is **heart-warming** makes you feel happier and more confident in other people.

His case is a remarkable and heart-warming story of care and devotion.

1.49 See also **warm**: 10.17–10.22.

-hearted

1.50 **-hearted** combines with adjectives such as 'warm' and 'generous' to produce words which describe someone's character or behaviour towards other people. Below are explanations of some of the most common words formed in this way, and a list giving further examples of adjectives that are often combined with **-hearted**.

1.51 Someone who is **big-hearted** is generous and kind.

The big-hearted fighter forgave his opponent and reassured him he was not to blame for the injuries.

1.52 Someone who is **faint-hearted** is not brave enough to do dangerous things.

Our groups must be totally self-sufficient. This is not a journey for the faint-hearted.

1.53 If you describe an event as **half-hearted**, you mean that people are not trying their best to make it successful, or are not very interested in it.

There was a half-hearted attempt at singing to keep up our spirits.
It was a half-hearted affair compared to the celebrations in the weeks after liberation.

1.54 If you give something **whole-hearted** support or agreement, you support or agree with it completely and enthusiastically.

He enjoys the whole-hearted support and affection of his own people.

1.55 Here are some more examples of words formed in this way:

cold-hearted	kind-hearted	tender-hearted
down-hearted	light-hearted	tough-hearted
generous-hearted	open-hearted	warm-hearted
gentle-hearted	soft-hearted	
hard-hearted	stout-hearted	

hand

1.56 **Hands** are associated with helping and taking part in something. If you **give** or **lend** someone **a hand**, you help them to do something. If you **need a hand** with something, you need help with it.

Look, could you give me a hand?
Friends and neighbours gave a hand.
Visitors would help with potato picking and harvesting. Everyone lent a hand.
'Do come along in case I need a hand,' he said.
When you're decorating professional advice comes in useful, so Ideal Home is offering you a helping hand.

1.57 If you **have a hand in** an event or project, you take part in its organization.

Britain's Stonewall Group had a hand in the report.
The President has accused these people of having a hand in the killing.

1.58 A **hands-on** way of doing things is an approach that involves direct experience and contact. For example, someone with a **hands-on** approach to government or business likes to be personally involved with all decisions. A **hands-on** approach to working or learning places importance on becoming as closely involved as possible with practical issues.

They already make a very hands-on contribution to the running of the house and the race-track.

*This stimulating book places great emphasis on an enjoyable
hands-on approach to learning.*
*You'll be expected to have a degree, a teacher-training qual-
ification and a few years of hands-on experience.*

1.59 A **hands-off** way of doing things is an approach that does not
involve working closely with practical issues. For example, if someone runs a government or a company with a **hands-off** approach, they
prefer to leave many of the decisions to other people.

*The administration has opted for a hands-off approach to foreign
exchange.*
*The government feared a hands-off policy would bring still more
unemployment and social tension in the East.*

stomach

1.60 People often find that unpleasant things that they see or smell
make them feel sick, and because of this, the **stomach** and **sickness**
are associated with reactions to unpleasant things. **Stomach** is used
in several expressions which show that you find something you may
have to do very unpleasant.

See also **sick, sickness: 2.15–2.19**.

1.61 If you **cannot stomach** something, you refuse to take part in it
or do it because you find it unpleasant or think it is wrong. If you
cannot stomach a fact or an idea, you cannot accept that it is true,
because it is against your own beliefs.

I could stomach no more and got out.
*It seems he could not stomach another discussion about the
islands.*
*They simply cannot stomach what economic success means: some
people getting richer than others.*

1.62 If you **do not have the stomach** for doing something or to do
something, you refuse to do it, or find it very difficult to do because
you find it very unpleasant or think that it is wrong.

*He asked me to go and clear out the attic of any important papers
as he hadn't the stomach for it.*
You've never had any stomach for fighting this man.
They had no stomach to fire on the demonstrators.

guts

1.63 A person's or animal's **guts** are all the organs inside their
abdomen. **Guts** is used metaphorically to refer to someone's strength
of character and determination. If you say that someone has **guts**, you
mean that they have courage and are prepared to fight for themselves

or for what they believe in. This is used more frequently in spoken English than in writing.

She has guts, which is unusual in a young actress.
You do not need capital to start in business; you need guts and the absolute belief that you will succeed.

1.64 If you have the **guts** to say or do something, you have enough courage to say or do it even though you know that it is dangerous or that people will disapprove of you if you do it.

I had the guts to say things to him that she didn't dare say.
It takes a lot of guts to come here on your own.

1.65 If you say that you **hate** someone's **guts**, you mean that you hate them very much. This is an informal expression.

I hated him, hated his guts for what he'd done to Rose.
He won't get a penny out of her. She hates his guts.

1.66 If you **work**, **slog**, or **fight** your **guts out**, you put all your time and energy into working for something. This is an informal use.

These women were amazing. They worked their guts out from 7.30 to 4.30 every day, often all evening and weekend too.
Those of us who are still working are slogging our guts out to pay for you and your blunders.
He had fought his guts out for that house so that he could give his family a lovely place to grow up.

1.67 If you **run** your **guts out**, you run as fast as you possibly can, so that you become completely exhausted. This is an informal use.

...the disappointment of the World Championships last year, in which he ran his guts out and finished fourth.

blood

1.68 Your **blood** is the liquid that flows inside your body, supplying oxygen and other vital substances. In former times, it was believed that the substances in your blood affected your character and your emotions, and that people of a high social class had better characters because they had better blood. Nowadays, people know that this is not true, but **blood** is still often used to refer to people's emotions, and to qualities which are seen as being related to their social or racial origins.

1.69 Negative feelings such as resentment, hate, and anger can be referred to as **bad blood**.

Both men worked in the printshop of the New York Financial Chronicle and there had been <u>bad blood</u> between them for some time.

<u>Bad blood</u> has arisen between our two daughters because each wants us to retire to their town.

1.70 If a crime is committed **in cold blood**, it is not done under the influence of strong emotion, and may have been planned.

They murdered my brother. They shot him down <u>in cold blood</u>.

See also **cold-blooded: 1.77**.

1.71 If you say that someone has, for example, **English blood** or **African blood**, you mean that either or both of their parents were English or African.

My father regretted that he himself had no Jewish <u>blood</u>.
He's got Spanish <u>blood</u> in him.

1.72 If you say that an ability or quality is **in** someone's **blood**, you mean that it is part of their nature.

Acting is <u>in</u> her <u>blood</u>.
I am a man of the countryside. It is <u>in my blood</u>.

1.73 If you are related to someone by **blood**, you are related to them by birth, rather than by adoption or marriage.

He will be your husband's closest <u>blood</u> relative.
...a man who is no relation by <u>blood</u> or adoption but who, after an astonishing court ruling, has won custody of the little boy.

1.74 See also **boil: 7.34, freeze: 10.80**.

-blooded

1.75 **-blooded** combines with the adjectives 'hot', 'cold', and 'red' to form words which describe someone's character. These words are explained below. Note that **-blooded** is not combined with any other adjectives in this way.

1.76 **Hot-blooded** emotions are strong, powerful feelings. **Hot-blooded** people have very strong emotions.

...<u>hot-blooded</u> passion.
Coppola is one of our more <u>hot-blooded</u> directors.

1.77 If you describe an action as **cold-blooded**, you mean that it is not done under the influence of strong emotion and may have been planned.

They stand accused of the <u>cold-blooded</u> murder of their parents.

See also **cold blood: 1.70**.

Note that **cold-blooded** is also a scientific term used to describe animals which do not maintain a constant, relatively high body temperature.

1.78 If someone says that a man is **red-blooded**, they mean that he is strong and healthy and seems to show a strong interest in sex. This is an informal expression.

> *As she posed for our photographer, passing drivers, local shopkeepers, in fact just about any <u>red-blooded</u> male in the vicinity, contorted their necks to get a look at her.*

1.79 Warm-blooded is a scientific term which is used to describe animals which maintain a relatively high, constant body temperature. It is not used metaphorically.

Bones

1.80 Your **bones** are the strong, hard things that support your body and together form your skeleton. The following words for bones are used metaphorically, especially to refer to the structure or outline of something and refer to instinctive feelings, strength, and courage.

bone

1.81 If you say that something that someone says or writes is **close to the bone**, you mean that although it is unpleasant it is true, and so makes you feel upset or uncomfortable. This comes from the idea that if you cut yourself so deeply that you can see the bone beneath your skin, it is very serious and painful.

> *Guibert's realism may be somewhat <u>close to the bone</u> for those who prefer to keep a distance from the subject they are reading about.*
> *Because its themes are old age and death, he said it was too <u>close to the bone</u>.*

1.82 If something is **cut** or **pared to the bone**, it is reduced by so much that only the essential parts are left, and no more could be taken from it without destroying it.

> *Most firms seem to agree that the key is to cut variable costs <u>to the bone</u>, but keep long-term investments intact.*
> *Universities feel they have already been <u>pared to the bone</u> by government cuts.*
> *We've seen throughout the last three or four years major job losses throughout the finance industry. We are down <u>to the bone</u>.*

1.83 If you say that you **know** or **feel in your bones** that something is that case, you mean that you feel sure that it is the case even though there is no evidence to support you.

> *Nothing made any sense except I <u>knew in my bones</u> that something was badly wrong.*
> *I <u>felt in my bones</u> that this letter would need to be correct in every detail.*

skeleton

1.84 Your **skeleton** is the frame of your body, which supports the rest of it. Without your skeleton, you could not move and your body would not be able to work properly. **Skeleton** is used metaphorically to talk about the most important or fundamental part of something.

The **skeleton staff** of an organization is the minimum number of people who can keep it functioning. The **skeleton** of a piece of writing is an early version which only contains the most important ideas.

> *There was still a <u>skeleton staff</u>; nursing auxiliaries, ward maids, kitchen hands.*
> *...the <u>skeleton</u> of his plan.*

backbone

1.85 Your **backbone** is the long series of small bones that runs down your back, from your neck to your pelvis. These are the most important bones in your body, as they allow you to move freely and also carry important messages from the rest of your body to your brain along millions of nerves. Because of this, your backbone is very important. **Backbone** is used metaphorically to talk about something that is a very important part of a large structure.

1.86 If you say that a person or a group of people is the **backbone** of an organization or country, you mean that they provide most of its strength and effectiveness, and that without them the group or organization would not be able to work as well as it does.

> *In Britain small businesses are the <u>backbone</u> of the Asian community.*
> *Women are the church's <u>backbone</u> but rarely hold any positions of leadership.*
> *The main trade union federation lost its <u>backbone</u> after 23,000 miners were sacked in 1986.*

1.87 If you say that someone **has backbone**, you mean that they have the courage to do things which they think are necessary even in difficult or dangerous situations.

> *The men of his time <u>had</u> more <u>backbone</u>.*
> *What can a wife do <u>if</u> her husband <u>has</u> no <u>backbone</u>?*

spineless

1.88 Your **spine** is the same as your **backbone**. **Spine** is rarely used metaphorically but the idea of your spine being the part of your body that supports you and gives you strength is used in the word **spineless**.

If you describe someone as **spineless**, you mean that you think that they lack strength and courage, and are therefore weak and likely to be easily influenced by other people.

> *I feel a bit stupid and spineless for not having stood my ground.*
> *...spineless idiots who are looking for an easy dollar.*

Processes in your body

1.89 This section deals with words for some processes which take place within the human body and which are used metaphorically to refer to other processes.

digest

1.90 When you **digest** food that you have eaten, the chemicals in your stomach break it down so that your body can absorb the substances it needs and get rid of the rest. If you say that you **digest** something such as news or information, you mean that after you have heard or read it, you think about it until you understand it.

> *There was another delay as Armstrong digested the information.*
> *He will have digested the news that there are to be no cash handouts.*
> *The financial community here in Britain has been digesting the latest inflation figures.*

Note that the noun **digestion** is not used in this way.

swallow

1.91 When you **swallow** something such as food or drink, you cause it to go from your mouth down to your stomach. **Swallow** is used metaphorically in two different ways: one is to talk about whether or not someone believes a piece of information, and the other is to talk about having to conceal emotions.

1.92 If you say that someone **swallows** a story or information, you mean that they seem to believe it, even though it seems to you that it is very unlikely to be true.

> *I swallowed his story because it gave me the chance to prove myself.*

1.93 If you find a fact or a story difficult to believe because it is so strange, unlikely, or unpleasant, you can say that you find it hard **to swallow**.

The police said they think it's a hard story to swallow.
Some of the penalties can be hard to swallow.
It's difficult to swallow what she's done to this family.

1.94 If someone finds advice **hard to swallow**, they do not want to accept it because they do not like it or because the advice they are being given is not what they expected.

Haig would have found this advice very hard to swallow.

1.95 If someone has to **swallow** feelings that they have, such as anger, they have to try to pretend they do not have them, or they have to try not to let them affect their behaviour.

Grossman swallowed his impatience, and began his lecture once again.
I swallowed my disappointment quickly.
The deputies are being asked to swallow their national pride and back down.

2 Health and Illness

2.1 Many words which refer to health, illness, and injury are used metaphorically. This chapter looks at some of the most common of these, beginning with words such as **healthy** and **unhealthy**, which are used to talk about how fit someone is and whether or not they are suffering from an illness or injury, moving on to words related to specific illnesses such as **cancer**. Next, various words used to talk about physical disabilities and disabled people are discussed, and finally this chapter looks at words related to damage to your body such as **wound** and **hurt**.

Health

health

2.2 Your **health** is how physically fit you are and whether or not you are ill or likely to become ill.

Health is sometimes used to refer to an organization's financial situation, and whether or not they have enough money to pay for all the things they need or to do all the things they want.

> A corporation's annual report supposedly presents a clear, precise picture of the financial status or <u>health</u> of the company.
> We were allowed to do anything which was beneficial to the <u>health</u> of the business.

Health is used much less commonly as a metaphor than **healthy**.

healthy

2.3 If a person is **healthy**, they are physically fit and are not suffering from any illnesses. **Healthy** is used metaphorically in several ways to indicate whether something such as a situation, organization, or relationship is good or positive.

2.4 If the financial situation of a person, organization, or country is **healthy**, that person, organization, or country has plenty of money for their needs and is therefore likely to be able to pay for all the things they need or to do all the things they want.

> Tom resigned, but with a very <u>healthy</u> bank account in his name he didn't worry too much about the future.
> China's economy has shown <u>healthy</u> growth in the first half of this year.
> The conservatives believe that lower taxes create a <u>healthier</u> economy and more growth.

2.5 If a company has **healthy** profits, it makes large profits, so that it is able to pay all its expenses and still have a lot of money left over.

In a wise move before their record's success, the band bought back their publishing rights, and sold them on to EMI for a <u>healthy</u> profit.
Wycombe has <u>healthier</u> finances and better facilities than most football clubs of modest means.

2.6 If you describe someone's feelings as **healthy**, you think they are appropriate to the situation that they are in, and that that person is showing understanding and good sense.

<u>Healthy</u> self-esteem should not be confused with self-centredness.
But if you listen to the nice people in the village, you'll get a much more objective, balanced and <u>healthy</u> view.
Arguing need not be destructive but can be a <u>healthy</u> way of resolving issues.

2.7 A **healthy** relationship is one in which both partners respect each other and feel that the relationship allows each of them opportunities to develop in their own way.

If you have a good and <u>healthy</u> relationship with your children, these problems can be minimized and talked about.
It should be possible to start rebuilding your relationship on a <u>healthier</u> basis.

2.8 A **healthy society** is a society that people think is good and desirable, for example because there is little crime and people have equal opportunities.

Arnold argued for a concept of equality as the basis of a <u>healthy</u> society.

unhealthy

2.9 If you are **unhealthy**, you are not physically fit, and may be ill or likely to become ill. **Unhealthy** is used metaphorically to indicate that something such as a situation, organization, or relationship is bad or negative.

2.10 If you describe a situation as **unhealthy**, you think that it is not normal or desirable and that it is likely to have bad effects. If you describe someone's feelings as **unhealthy**, you think that they are inappropriate to a particular situation, and that they might have bad effects.

Jealousy has its roots in <u>unhealthy</u> patterns of development.
Organised crime is now taking an <u>unhealthy</u> interest in computer fraud.
There are many who feel that it is <u>unhealthy</u> for a nation to carry on constantly electing the same party.

2.11 An **unhealthy** financial situation is one in which people are losing money and business affairs seem to be out of control.

> *The enforced redundancy of skilled and experienced workers is a clear sign of an <u>unhealthy</u> economy.*
> *They have been hearing details of the club's <u>unhealthy</u> financial position, falling membership and declining income.*

Illnesses

2.12 Words which are used to describe illnesses are also often used metaphorically to talk about the condition of societies or groups of people when these are bad or seem to be becoming bad.

ills

2.13 If someone is not healthy or is suffering from an illness, you can say that they are **ill**. Ill is not used as a metaphor in this way, but the plural form of the noun **ills** is used to refer to things that cause problems or difficulties in an organization or society. When it is used in this way, **ills** usually occurs after an adjective or is followed by **of** and a noun.

> *...in pursuit of a cure for the country's economic <u>ills</u>.*
> *National Service is one method of putting people to work on America's social <u>ills</u>.*
> *Politicians are being blamed for all the <u>ills of</u> society.*

Note that the noun **illness** is not usually used metaphorically.

ailing

2.14 If someone is **ailing**, they are ill and do not seem to be getting better. This is an old-fashioned use. An **ailing** organization or society has a lot of problems, especially financial problems, and it seems unlikely that things will improve. This use is most common in journalism.

> *Few of them have the qualifications or experience to put an <u>ailing</u> company back on its feet.*
> *Observers here believe that the greatest difficulty before him is the <u>ailing</u> economy of the country.*
> *It could also prove a disaster for many of the <u>ailing</u> British hotels and tourist attractions that rely heavily on American holiday-makers.*

sick

2.15 If you are **sick**, you are ill. **Sick** is used metaphorically to describe situations or behaviour which are bad or undesirable.

2.16 A **sick** organization, company, or economy has a lot of serious problems, especially financial problems. This use is most common in journalism.

> In 1980 the country was one of the world's biggest debtors and had a _sick_ economy; without relief it cured itself, repaid the debts and can now raise foreign capital.
> The fact is that _sick_ companies can't afford to do this.

2.17 If you describe a person or their behaviour as **sick**, you mean that they seem to show an unpleasant and unacceptable interest in death and suffering, or that they seem to enjoy behaving in a way that is likely to cause suffering.

> ...those _sick_ idiots who have written hateful things in letters and shouted stupid things at us in the street.
> Mr Leonard said, 'I have rejected this _sick_ society for an alternative lifestyle.'

2.18 If you describe something such as a joke or a story as **sick**, you mean that you think it deals with death or suffering in an unpleasant and frivolous way.

> To the thousands of people who've lost their life savings in branches abroad, it could sound like a _sick_ joke.
> That's really _sick_.

sickness

2.19 The noun **sickness** can be used with the same meanings as **sick**. **Sickness** is used in this way less frequently than **sick**.

> He has been at the centre of politics for too long to escape responsibility for the state's deeper _sicknesses_.
> He told her that her belief was part of a general _sickness_ of the modern mind, a _sickness_ that was also producing fascism and some forms of communism.

disease

2.20 A **disease** is an illness which affects people, animals, or plants, making them weaker and less healthy, and sometimes causing death.

You can refer to people's attitudes or practices as a **disease** when you think that they are harmful or wrong and likely to have bad effects or cause suffering. This is a fairly formal use.

The crippling <u>disease</u> of state involvement in industry through nationalisation has not been cured.
I have yet to meet a single American who automatically thinks any foreign product must be better than his own. The <u>disease</u> seems to be uniquely British.

Words related to illnesses

symptom

2.21 The **symptoms** of an illness are the physical signs that indicate that someone has that illness. For example, a red rash on your body is a symptom of the illness measles. Problems and bad situations are often talked about as if they were illnesses or diseases, and it is also possible to refer to the things that indicate that a problem or a bad situation exists as **symptoms** of that problem or situation.

Concern about law and order can, of course, be a <u>symptom</u> of social anxiety, or resistance to change.
I think it's a <u>symptom</u> of the rebellion and dissatisfaction of the youngsters in our society who are growing up.
The debate around the law is a <u>symptom</u> of a bigger problem.
There are other <u>symptoms</u> of decline.

symptomatic

2.22 If something is **symptomatic** of an illness, it is a physical sign that someone has that illness. If you say that something is **symptomatic** of a problem or a bad situation, you mean that it is a sign that that problem or bad situation exists.

This behaviour was <u>symptomatic</u> of a generally uncaring attitude towards his wife.
To some critics, the administration's troubles are <u>symptomatic</u> of something deeper.

syndrome

2.23 A **syndrome** is a medical condition that is characterized by a particular group of signs or symptoms. You can refer to an undesirable condition or situation that is characterized by a particular type of activity or behaviour as a particular **syndrome**.

If we look at history, what has happened at NATO is not unusual; I call it the rearview mirror <u>syndrome</u>.
I don't expect men to join the guilt-driven overwork <u>syndrome</u> we career women somehow accept.

The plural form **syndromes** is not usually used in this way.

infectious

2.24 A disease that is **infectious** can be caught by being near people who are infected with it. Most of the words associated with illness have a negative meaning when they are used metaphorically. However, when **infectious** is used as a metaphor, it has a positive meaning.

You can use **infectious** to describe a happy mood, smile, or laugh that makes other people feel happy too. It is interesting to compare this with **contagious (2.25)**, which is used in a similar way to describe both positive and negative emotions and feelings.

> *He has authority, strong skills of presentation and <u>infectious</u> enthusiasm and a sense of fun.*
> *...an <u>infectious</u> grin that immediately puts you at ease.*
> *...an <u>infectious</u> smile.*

Other words beginning with **infect-** such as **infected** and **infection** are rarely used metaphorically.

contagious

2.25 A disease that is **contagious** can be caught by touching people or things that are infected with it. When **contagious** is used metaphorically, it is used in a similar way to **infectious**, above, but it can be used about both positive and negative feelings and emotions.

You can use **contagious** to describe emotions and ideas which are passed from one person to another.

> *Their excitement was <u>contagious</u>, even over the telephone.*
> *He has told me his plans and he's made a good impression on me; his enthusiasm is <u>contagious</u>.*
> *Sometimes when you are afraid it becomes <u>contagious</u>, and the people around you begin to be afraid too.*

contagion

2.26 **Contagion** is the spread of a disease by coming into contact with a person or thing that has been infected with it. You can use **contagion** to refer to the spread of ideas between groups of people, especially when you want to show that you think that this is a bad thing. This is a fairly formal use.

> *...the <u>contagion</u> of ignorance that appeared to be spreading through the nation's young people.*
> *President Kim Il-Sung is determined to continue to insulate his country from the <u>contagion</u> of foreign ideas.*

fatal

2.27 A **fatal** illness or accident is one which causes death. People often use **fatal** as a metaphor to describe something which has very serious and negative results, such as a company closing.

> These firms are already suffering from the US recession and a further hike in duty could be a _fatal_ blow.
> No one in the family took Margaret's side. She had made a _fatal_ error; it was a terrible attack on Frances's deep religious faith.
> The mistake was _fatal_ to my plans.

2.28 **Fatal** is also used in a light-hearted way to say that something is very bad.

> She says. 'I like clothes and I love shopping and that's a _fatal_ combination.'
> Don't talk to your friends whatever you do. It's _fatal_ if you start talking about what you're going to do.
> ...that _fatal_ combination of socks with sandals.

deadly

2.29 If something is **deadly**, it is likely or able to cause someone's death, or has already caused someone's death. **Deadly** can be used metaphorically to emphasize that a situation is extremely serious or is likely to have a damaging effect. For example, a **deadly** error is likely to cause a very serious accident or problem; if someone says that they are **deadly** serious about something that they say, they are emphasizing that what they are saying is true, even though it is extremely unpleasant or undesirable.

> He wasn't laughing now. His face was _deadly_ serious.
> 'You must be joking,' Hunter said. 'Believe you me, old boy, I'm being _deadly_ earnest.'
> When one investment banker describes another as lacking in greed, that's a _deadly_ insult.

2.30 Something that is **deadly boring** or **deadly** is extremely boring. This is an informal use.

> The broadcast news was accurate and reliable but _deadly dull_.
> I leapt into the first secretarial job I could find, which was in the City and _deadly boring_.
> She finds these parties _deadly_.

pain

2.31 **Pain** is the feeling of great discomfort you have when you are ill or injured. This idea of suffering and discomfort is used metaphorically to talk about actions or feelings which have a bad effect on people.

2.32 You can refer to feelings of great unhappiness as **pain**.

> ...grey eyes that seemed filled with <u>pain</u>.
> She hid her <u>pain</u> and despair at the breakdown of the relation-ship from everyone.

2.33 Journalists sometimes refer to economic hardship as **pain**, especially when they want to emphasize that a lot of people are likely to suffer as a result of it.

> His economic reforms brought more <u>pain</u> than progress.
> With the unemployment rate standing at only 2.1%, most house-holds are feeling relatively little <u>pain</u>.
> The recession is causing too much <u>pain</u> and wrecking too many lives.

2.34 **Pain** is sometimes used as a verb with this meaning, although this is not common.

> It will also <u>pain</u> the corporate borrowers, to whom the cost will be passed on.

painful

2.35 If a part of your body is **painful**, it hurts, for example because it is injured or because there is something wrong with it. A **painful** illness or injury causes a great deal of pain and discomfort. **Painful** is used metaphorically in a similar way to **pain**, above, to say that something causes great hardship or suffering.

2.36 You can describe a situation, fact, or problem as **painful** when it is likely to upset people or cause great unhappiness.

> She would have to end the affair, however <u>painful</u> that experience might be.
> ...one of the most <u>painful</u> decisions of my career.

2.37 Journalists sometimes describe a situation in which people or companies are suffering financially as **painful**, especially when they want to emphasize that a lot of people are likely to suffer as a result of it.

> The governor of the Bank of England said that British companies faced a <u>painful</u> adjustment process ahead.
> The transition to a market economy will be slow and <u>painful</u>.
> It would not be possible without a series of other ambitious and <u>painful</u> reforms which include the selling-off of factories and farms.

hurt

2.38 If something **hurts** you, it causes you pain. If a part of your body **hurts**, you feel pain there. **Hurt** is used metaphorically to show that a situation, plan, or action causes people hardship or suffering.

2.39 If something that someone says or does **hurts** you, it makes you feel very unhappy or upset.

> *She's afraid that she is going to be hurt and that she'll never fall in love again.*
> *It hurts me to see people so demoralized.*

See also **wound: 2.62**.

2.40 Journalists sometimes say that something such as a new tax **hurts** people or businesses, or that it **hurts**, if it puts people or businesses in a worse economic position than they were in before, so that they suffer or are damaged.

> *Cuts in welfare could hurt the poor more than an energy tax.*
> *Interest rates, already high, will need to stay higher than inflation, hurting investment.*
> *The undervalued rouble is pushing up import prices and hurting the economy.*
> *The trouble now is that his policy may be hurting but not working effectively.*

fever

2.41 If you are ill and you have a **fever**, you have a very high temperature and your heart is beating more quickly than usual. **Fever** is used metaphorically to refer to situations which make people feel nervous or excited.

2.42 You can refer to extreme excitement or agitation about something as a **fever of** activity, especially when you want to suggest that you do not think that this is a good thing.

> *...the fever of expectation the film has already generated.*
> *He was in a fever of impatience.*

2.43 If activities reach **fever pitch**, they get to a point of great excitement and interest.

> *In the US, the top prizes go up to 20 million dollars, with excitement reaching fever pitch as the lottery grows each week it is unclaimed.*
> *The speculation reached fever pitch in 1987.*

feverish

2.44 If you are **feverish**, you are suffering from a fever. **Feverish** is used metaphorically in a similar way to **fever**, to suggest that an emotion or activity is extremely intense.

If you say that someone does something in a **feverish** way, you mean that they do it quickly and are excited and emotional, rather than calm, usually because it is important that they finish what they are doing as soon as possible.

> ...the _feverish_ arms race during the twenty years before August 1914.
>
> Scientists are working at a _feverish_ pace.
>
> ..._feverish_ publicity and speculation.

feverishly

2.45 If someone does something **feverishly**, they do it in a way that is excited or emotional, rather than calm, usually because it is important that they finish what they are doing as soon as possible.

> As Christmas approaches, publishers _feverishly_ push out new books.
>
> His mind worked _feverishly_, analysing the concept.
>
> They had talked hurriedly, _feverishly_, on the Sunday evening.

Words for particular illnesses

anaemic

2.46 If you are **anaemic**, you are suffering from a condition called anaemia, which means that you do not have enough iron in your blood. This makes you look pale and feel very weak and tired. This idea of weakness and being unable to do very much is used metaphorically to describe actions or processes which seem weak or ineffective.

> The film is a competent but _anaemic_ rehash of John Grisham's novel.
>
> An _anaemic_ recovery has created jobs, but only 800,000 of them.

Note that this is spelt **anemic** in American English.

> Most of that economic growth has been too _anemic_ to produce new jobs.

cancer

2.47 Cancer is a serious disease in which cells in a person's body reproduce rapidly and in an uncontrolled way, producing abnormal growths. Until recently, nearly all cancers were fatal, and it is still considered to be a very dangerous disease.

If you describe something as a **cancer,** you mean that you think it is extremely evil and unpleasant and will have bad and dangerous effects. This is a formal use.

> We cannot surrender the streets of our cities to the _cancer_ of racism and fascism.
> They have helped conquer the _cancer_ of apartheid that looked like tearing their country apart.
> We have to take a stand against racism. It is a _cancer_ sweeping across Europe.

Note that when **cancer** is used with its literal meaning, it is usually an uncount noun, and that when it is used with its metaphorical meaning, it is usually a count noun.

jaundiced

2.48 Jaundice is an illness which makes your skin and eyes turn yellow. **Jaundice** is rarely used metaphorically. The related word, **jaundiced**, which is an old-fashioned way of describing someone who is suffering from jaundice, is now used much more commonly as a metaphor than it is with its literal meaning.

Jaundiced is used to describe people's attitudes or feelings. Someone who has a **jaundiced** view of something is unenthusiastic about it, often because they are tired or have had discouraging experiences.

> Reg observed these preparations with a _jaundiced_ eye.
> ...a _jaundiced_ view of American society.
> ...a _jaundiced_ television executive.

headache

2.49 If you have a **headache**, you feel unwell because your head hurts. A headache is most commonly caused because you are tired or worried, and although it is unpleasant and inconvenient, it is usually something you have to suffer until it goes away.

You can refer to a problem that causes you anxiety over a period of time and cannot easily be solved as a **headache**. **Headache** is usually used in this way to refer to problems that are not very serious but that irritate or worry you.

> The biggest _headache_ for mothers hoping to return to study is childcare.
> Financial problems have been a constant _headache_ for the Centre's directors.
> The airline's biggest _headache_ is the sharp increase in the price of aviation fuel, up by 23% between June and September.

Lenders like real estate because there's little risk, and mortgages have historically offered reasonable returns with few administrative headaches.

Note that **headache** is not usually used in this way to refer to a single, sudden event, such as an accident.

rash

2.50 A **rash** is an area of red spots that appears on your skin because you are ill or allergic to something. You can refer to a number of similar things that happen or occur around the same time as **a rash of** those things. **Rash** is usually used in this way to describe things which are considered unpleasant or undesirable, but it can also be used ironically or humorously.

There was a rash of burglaries among the summer cottages.
...a rash of murders in London's East End.
Preparations for next year's Olympic Games have led to a rash of building sites.
In the 1970s, a rash of new publications hit the stands.

Note that the plural form **rashes** is not used in this way.

Physical disability

2.51 Many of the words used to talk about physical disability are also used metaphorically to talk about things being damaged or about damage becoming worse.

cripple

2.52 A **cripple** is a person who has a physical disability. This word was common in former times, but is now considered to be offensive when it is used with this meaning. It is still used metaphorically, however, to refer to someone who has a mental or social problem that prevents them from living a normal, happy life. For example, if you say that someone is an **emotional cripple**, you think that they are psychologically damaged in a way that stops them from understanding and expressing their emotions normally.

When **cripple** is used in this way, it must come after an adjective such as 'emotional'.

You may read my story and say I was an emotional cripple.
If, from my letter, you have judged me to be an emotional cripple who is incapable of forming normal relationships, you are wrong.
The people using these agencies are not social cripples; a large proportion of them are successful young professionals.

2.53 If an illness or an accident **cripples** someone, it causes them to have a serious and permanent physical disability. Note that, unlike the literal use of the noun discussed above, the literal use of the verb **cripple** is not considered old-fashioned or offensive. This idea of permanent serious damage is used metaphorically to describe an event or problem that damages a person or organization so severely that it becomes impossible for them to function normally.

Cripple is often used in this way by journalists to talk about businesses, financial matters, and the economy.

> *A rich man can ignore losses that <u>would cripple</u> someone who isn't wealthy.*
> *...the crisis of high interest rates and high exchange rates which <u>crippled</u> British industry.*
> *His business <u>was crippled</u> by debts.*

2.54 If someone is **emotionally crippled** by something unpleasant that happens to them, they suffer so much as a result of this that they become psychologically damaged in a way that stops them from understanding and expressing their emotions normally.

> *The horrific costs can leave couples financially devastated and <u>emotionally crippled</u>.*
> *I'm not perfect but I'm also not <u>emotionally crippled</u>.*

crippling

2.55 A **crippling** illness or disease causes severe and permanent physical damage. **Crippling** is used metaphorically to describe a problem or an event which stops a person or an organization from being able to work properly, and will probably cause them to fail completely.

If a person or an organization suffers a **crippling blow**, an event damages them so much that it is almost impossible for them to recover.

> *Leeds were near the bottom of Division Two and facing <u>crippling</u> debts.*
> *...<u>crippling</u> court costs and legal fees.*
> *In the 1950s movie theaters suffered a <u>crippling blow</u> as television sets made their way into more and more homes, offering entertainment at no charge.*

paralyse

2.56 If someone **is paralysed** by an accident or an illness, they have no feeling in their body, or in a part of their body, and are unable to move. **Paralyse** is used metaphorically to talk about something that causes a person, place, system, or organization to be unable to function at all. For example, if you **are paralysed** by fear, you are so frightened that you are unable to move; if a factory **is paralysed** by a strike, the strike causes the factory to shut down completely and stop producing goods.

> He _was_ suddenly _paralysed_ by fear.
> Much of industry and business on the island _is paralysed_ by a general strike.
> ...causing a traffic jam that stretched all the way back to Heathrow Airport, _paralysing_ the city.
> Fear of unemployment _is paralysing_ the economy.

Note that this is spelt **paralyze** in American English.

> It's hoped that this snowfall _won't paralyze_ the region the way last week's did.
> I _was_ never _paralyzed_ by depression.

paralysed, paralysing

2.57 The adjectives formed from the verb **paralyse**, **paralysed** and **paralysing**, are used to talk about events or actions that stop things from working efficiently or being successful. For example, a **paralysed** economy is very weak and events have made it impossible for it to improve; a **paralysing** strike causes a factory or even a whole section of the economy to be unable to function at all.

> ...a _paralysed_ economy.
> This has left the country with a _paralysed_ government at a time when it must react quickly if it is to survive.
> It's a relief that my bank has closed for the day and isn't going to phone again with another _paralysing_ demand for money.

Note that these adjectives are spelt **paralyzed**, **paralyzing** in American English.

> ...a _paralyzed_ communist party.
> Dave had a _paralyzing_ fear of Zuckerman.

paralysis

2.58 Paralysis is the state of being paralysed. **Paralysis** is used metaphorically in a similar way to **paralyse**, to show that something such as a place, system, or organization is unable to act or function in any way. **Paralysis** is often used in this way by journalists when they are talking about economics or politics.

> ...economic chaos and political _paralysis_.
> They are selling those few shares which still show gains and hanging on to those that would show losses. The result will soon be total _paralysis_.

lame

2.59 If a person is **lame**, they are unable to walk properly because an injury or illness has damaged one or both of their legs. In former times, when most jobs involved physical activity, a lame person would not have been considered to be as useful or effective as most other people.

Lame is used metaphorically to describe arguments, explanations, or excuses that are considered to be weak and unconvincing.

> *The news only made the president's initial response to the disaster seem more lame.*
> *He mumbled some lame excuse about having gone to sleep.*
> *These promises sound increasingly lame.*

limp

2.60 If someone **limps**, they walk in a slow and awkward way because they have hurt or injured one or both of their legs. If you say that something such as an activity or a process **limps along**, or **limps**, you mean that it continues to exist or function, but with obvious difficulty.

> *Their share prices have limped along.*
> *The discussion limped to inevitable collapse.*
> *The department's workload has tripled in the past ten years. It limps along hopelessly understaffed.*

Injuries

2.61 Many words used to talk about physical injury are also used metaphorically to talk about non-physical damage to people, systems, and organizations.

wound

2.62 A **wound** is damage to part of your body, especially a hole or tear in your flesh, caused by a weapon or something sharp. **Wound** is used metaphorically to talk about damage that one person causes to another person's reputation or feelings, especially when you want to suggest that this has been caused deliberately, or by carelessness that should have been avoided.

2.63 A **wound** is a lasting bad effect on someone's mind or feelings caused by insults or bad experiences. This is a literary use.

> *She has been so badly hurt it may take forever for the wounds to heal.*

2.64 If someone **licks** their **wounds**, they try to recover from a hurtful or damaging experience, usually by going somewhere quiet by themselves.

> She would go home for the weekend: she would retreat and lick her wounds a little.
> He'd been too busy licking his own wounds to notice what was happening to his mother.

2.65 If someone **heals** or **binds** their **wounds**, they recover from being hurt or defeated. If this expression is used about a group of people, the damage may be due to disagreements between themselves.

> Perhaps the Government can stop worrying about healing its own wounds and start tackling the economic mess this country is in.
> Future Tory support will depend not only on who wins the leadership contest but whether the party can bind its wounds afterwards.

2.66 If an **old wound is opened** or **reopened**, an incident causes people to feel pain and unhappiness about something that happened in the past.

> He had a decided impression that he was opening old wounds.
> On top of this, the old wounds in our community's relations with the police have been reopened by this recent tragic and horrible death.

2.67 If a weapon or something sharp **wounds** you, it damages your flesh. This verb is used metaphorically to talk about causing damage to a person's feelings, especially when you want to suggest that this is done deliberately, or by carelessness that should have been avoided.

If one person **wounds** another, the first person behaves in a thoughtless or unkind way, which makes the other person feel unhappy.

> His final, formal rejection of her offer in late May seemed calculated to wound.
> You don't mess with this lady. Her tongue can wound at times.
> The Chancellor has been wounded by some of the criticism of him and his handling of the economy.

wounded, wounding

2.68 The adjectives formed from the verb **wound**, **wounded** and **wounding**, are used to talk about actions or remarks that upset people. For example, if you feel **wounded** by something that someone has said or done, you feel very upset because of it; a **wounding** remark makes you feel very upset.

> Some parents merely want to help, and feel wounded when the adolescent says, 'No, thanks.'

But if that were all there was to it, his words would not have seemed so wounding.

bruise

2.69 A **bruise** is an injury which occurs as a yellowish-purple mark on your skin. If you **bruise** a part of your body, a bruise appears on it, for example because something hit you. **Bruise** is used metaphorically in a similar way to **wound** to talk about damage to a person's feelings.

2.70 If an incident or someone's behaviour **bruises** your feelings, it makes you feel unhappy, and means that you may find it difficult to trust people in the future.

Some women's self-esteem has been badly bruised.
...the bruised feelings of those he had insulted.
Her trust in him had been so bruised that she decided to keep him out of her office.

Note that the noun **bruise** is not usually used as a metaphor.

2.71 If you say that someone has a **bruised ego**, you are making fun of them, usually in a friendly way, because they thought that they were very important but something has happened that has upset their view of themselves.

It was, on the whole, a terrible day of criticism. Around every corner there were bruised egos.
We have a couple of injuries from this game but there were also a few bruised egos and broken hearts.

2.72 Journalists sometimes use **bruise** in a similar way to talk about damage in finance and politics. For example, if a company **is bruised** by an event, it becomes weaker or less successful because of this event.

The computer company has been badly bruised by the sudden switch to Windows.
The incident has left the central government's policy initiative badly bruised and its advisors shaken.

bruising

2.73 A **bruising** meeting or argument is one in which there are strong disagreements which leave people feeling upset or with their reputations damaged.

That is the crucial question in what looks set to turn into a bruising battle between the company and the union.
In some fundamental way, my trust in Alex had been impaired by that bruising interview.

Note that this adjective is not usually used to talk about something such as an injury which causes bruises to appear on someone's body.

scar

2.74 A **scar** is a mark on your skin left after an injury has healed. **Scars** are permanent, although they sometimes fade a little over a period of time. **Scar** is used metaphorically to talk about the effects that unpleasant experiences sometimes have on people.

2.75 If someone has had a bad experience which will affect them permanently or for a very long time, you can say that they carry **the scars of** that experience. This use is most common in written English.

> *On the outside I may seem to be fiercely independent, but on the inside I carry <u>the scars of</u> not having been accepted and loved for what I am.*
> *She carries <u>the</u> invisible <u>scars of</u> someone who knows all about pain.*

2.76 If someone **is scarred** by a bad experience, they will be affected by it permanently or for a very long time. This use is most common in written English.

> *But when she was 17 her life <u>was scarred</u> by the deaths of a brother and a sister within months of each other.*

3 Animals

3.1 A very large number of words used to talk about animals are also used metaphorically. This chapter only covers some of them, focusing on some of the most common ones. The chapter begins by looking at general words used to refer to animals, such as **animal** and **beast**. Then there are three sections on particular kinds of animals; **domestic animals**, **farm animals**, and **wild animals**.

General words for animals

3.2 Words such as **animal**, **beast**, and **brute** are often used as metaphors to talk about the way people behave, by suggesting that their behaviour is more like that of an animal than a person. These words are often, but not always, used in this way showing disapproval.

animal

3.3 If you say that someone is an **animal**, you find their behaviour disgusting and unacceptable, often because they are violent.

Whoever did this is a maniac, an <u>animal</u>.
He was an <u>animal</u> on Saturday afternoon and is a disgrace to English football.
He said, 'These people are <u>animals</u> and what they did was unforgivable.'

3.4 You can also use **animal** to show that you are talking about the physical nature of people, associated with their senses, instincts, or strength rather than with their personality or intelligence.

The human <u>animal</u> fights to protect its own life.
The labourer was a manufacturing <u>animal</u>, perceived solely as a source of profit.

3.5 If you refer to someone as a particular kind of **animal**, you mean that they enjoy that kind of activity and that they are naturally very good at it. For example, if you say that someone is **a social animal**, you mean that they enjoy the company of other people and enjoy social occasions.

'I'm a bit of a <u>social animal</u> and I enjoy company,' he says. 'I'm an extrovert.'
She had never struck me as a <u>political animal</u> and I don't think she was. She did what she had to in order to survive.

3.6 Animal passions or **animal instincts** are very strong feelings or instincts, such as strong sexual feelings, that are associated with your senses and instincts rather than with your personality or intelligence.

> *Newman lay back on the bed. It had been sheer <u>animal</u> passion.*
> *Like all great discoveries, I located it by pure <u>animal</u> instinct.*

Here are some examples of words commonly used after **animal** in this way:

aggression	impulse	passion
attraction	instinct	pleasure
desire	magnetism	strength
energy	nature	

beast

3.7 You can refer to an animal as a **beast**, especially if it is very large or very dangerous. **Beast** is used metaphorically in a similar way to **animal**.

3.8 If you call someone a **beast**, you find their behaviour disgusting or unacceptable, usually because they are violent.

> *After his marriage he became a drunk, a madman, a <u>beast</u>.*
> *A horrified pensioner who tried to save her said last night, 'I was trying to help her, pleading with them to stop, and a girl threatened to smash my face in. They were just <u>beasts</u>.'*
> *These were not men but <u>beasts</u> which had come out of the undergrowth. They had snatched his son. They were minutes away from killing him.*

3.9 Beast can also be used as an friendly, affectionate way of referring to someone, usually a man or boy, who you know very well, if they have been a little silly or bad.

> *Where is Richard, the little <u>beast</u>?*
> *I know he was a grumpy little <u>beast</u>, but I loved him.*

beastly

3.10 Beastly means very unpleasant. This is an old-fashioned word, used in informal spoken English.

> *'The main reason why I'm not married is because men are in general so utterly <u>beastly</u> to women,' she said.*
> *The weather was <u>beastly</u>.*

brute

3.11 In former times, **brute** was used in a similar way to **beast**, to refer to an animal, especially a very large or a very dangerous animal.

These days, this use is rare, and **brute** is more commonly used in the ways explained below.

3.12 If you refer to a man as a **brute**, you dislike him very much because he does not think about other people, and behaves in a violent and unpleasant way.

> *The man was a brute, he spent the little he earned on drink.*
> *That is why society must be protected from brutes like him.*

3.13 You can talk about **brute force** or **brute strength** to refer to strength that is purely physical, rather than power that comes from intelligence or skill.

> *They seem to think that brute force solves every problem.*
> *He stresses that his sport is very much a test of skill and technique rather than brute strength.*

brutish

3.14 If you describe a person or their behaviour as **brutish**, you think that they are violent or uncivilized.

> *...an insensitive and brutish husband.*
> *With brutish ferocity, he reached out both hands and locked his grip onto the handles of the trolley.*

prey

3.15 An animal's **prey** is the animals it catches and eats in order to survive. **Prey** can be used metaphorically to talk about people who seem likely to be taken advantage of or harmed by other people. For example, if one person **is prey to** another, the second person could easily harm or take advantage of the first, usually by deceiving them; if one person **falls prey** to another, the second person harms or takes advantage of the first person, often by deceiving them.

> *The miners will be prey to all sorts of people claiming to be financial experts.*
> *Tourists who take fistfuls of dollars to exchange are regarded as easy prey by thieves.*
> *Lonely secretaries fell prey to the charms of his agents.*

3.16 If you **are prey to** a particular kind of unpleasant feeling, you often feel unhappy because of that feeling.

> *'I'm not sure,' he answered truthfully, 'I'm prey to nagging doubts but that's not unusual, you know me.'*
> *His talent as a writer brought him success, yet he was prey to a growing despair.*
> *Although I don't fall prey to self-pity often, it does happen.*

3.17 An animal that **preys on** other animals survives by catching and eating them. This idea of one animal or group of animals surviving by killing another is used to talk about people who seem to become powerful or successful by harming or taking advantage of a particular person or group of people.

3.18 If you say that one person **preys on** or **preys upon** another, you mean that the first person uses their power or strength to take advantage of or harm the second person in some way.

> Tourists *are frequently preyed upon* by robbers who lurk outside Miami airport.
> He always struck at night and *preyed upon* single women living in ground floor flats in London and Essex.
> The survey claims loan companies *prey on* weak families already in debt.

3.19 If a worry or an unpleasant feeling **preys on** your **mind**, you have difficulty forgetting it, and it makes you nervous or unhappy.

> The policemen do not allow the risks to *prey on their minds*.
> There were other things, more important things, that *had been preying on* her *mind*.

Particular kinds of animals

3.20 This section is split into three groups: **domestic animals**; **farm animals**; and **wild animals**.

There are two common grammatical changes which occur within these groups of metaphors. Firstly, some of the names of animals can be used as verbs when they are used metaphorically, such as **pig**. These are explained after the noun that they relate to. In some cases, the verb is a more common metaphor than the noun. Secondly, there are some adjectives derived from names of animals, such as **tigerish**. These adjectives describe qualities which are associated with those animals; the corresponding noun is not always used metaphorically.

Domestic animals

3.21 This section looks at words for animals which are commonly kept as pets in Britain and the United States.

pet

3.22 A **pet** is an animal such as a dog or a cat that you keep in your home to give you company and pleasure. Animals that are kept as pets are usually well-treated and carefully looked after. **Pet** is used metaphorically to talk about a theory, idea, or subject which someone strongly believes in and supports. For example, someone's **pet project** is a project that they are very interested in and which they give more time and attention to than any other project; if you say that something is your **pet hate**, you mean that you dislike it intensely, often in a way that you realise other people will not understand or which they will find amusing.

When **pet** is used in this way, it must be followed by a noun.

She was heartily fed up with her husband's pet project.
His pet obsession is to computerise textbooks to make them faster, cheaper and more appealing to children.
He pauses before returning to his pet theory.
I can't think of any pet hates except perhaps game shows.

3.23 Some people call the person they are talking to '**pet**' to show affection and friendliness.

It's alright pet, let me do it.

dog

3.24 Dogs are very common pets in Britain and the United States, and are generally considered to be friendly, affectionate, and loyal animals. However, when **dog** is used as a metaphor, it is nearly always used to say negative things.

3.25 Some people use **dog** to refer to something which is of very poor quality. This is an informal use.

He said the old car was an absolute dog to drive.
The film must be a real dog.

3.26 If you say that a situation is **dog eat dog**, you mean that each person involved wants something for themselves, and is prepared to behave aggressively and hurt other people in order to get what they want.

It is very much dog eat dog out there.
We all have to make a living and there's no point in having a dog-eat-dog attitude.

3.27 If someone **is dogged** by something unpleasant, or if it **dogs** them, the unpleasant thing continues to affect them over a long period of time, and returns, possibly several times, after they think it has gone.

Controversy has dogged his career.
Her career has been dogged by ill-health over the past year.
He has been dogged by criticism ever since he came to prominence seven years ago.

dogged

3.28 If you describe people's character or actions as **dogged** (pronounced dogg–id), you mean that they are very persistent and refuse to give up even when there is a lot of opposition.

Miles succeeded at what he tackled with a combination of talent, dogged determination and a fine sense of humour.
He appeared unusually tired in the face of dogged questioning from the BBC's interviewer.

bitch

3.29 A **bitch** is a female dog. Although dogs are considered to be friendly animals, when **bitch** is used metaphorically it has very negative connotations.

3.30 If someone calls a woman a **bitch**, they are saying in a very rude way that they think that she is behaving aggressively or unpleasantly.

You are putting the men down and they don't like it, they think you are being a bitch.
Silly little bitch, what did she think she was playing at?
I'm very sorry I was a bitch.

3.31 Some people use **bitch** to refer to a situation which they find very unpleasant. This is an informal use which some people find offensive.

It's going to be a bitch to replace him.
It was a bitch of a winter that year.

3.32 If one person **bitches** about another person, the first person says unpleasant things about the second person when they are not present. People use **bitch** in this way to show that they disapprove of this behaviour.

Everyone was talking about property or inside deals between bitching about colleagues.
She bitched about Dan but I knew she was devoted to him.

hound

3.33 A **hound** is a type of dog that is specially bred and trained for hunting or racing. Hounds often have a highly developed sense of smell, and are able to follow animals that they are hunting for a very long time until they catch them. This idea of persistently following something is used in the verb **hound**.

3.34 If one person **hounds** another, the first person follows the second person in order to gain something from them in a way that the second person finds threatening or frightening.

> *I wish the press would leave them alone because if the marriage isn't breaking up, I feel it will do the way they are hounding them.*
> *I was only doing my job. I didn't hound him and I was only with him for about two or three minutes.*
> *She couldn't bear to return to the house, to the people hounding her.*

See also **hunt: 6.51–6.53**.

3.35 If people **hound** someone **out of** a position or place, they force that person to leave that position or place by criticizing them so much or by being so unpleasant to them it becomes impossible for them to stay there.

> *Sometimes I think that the government is going to hound us out of business.*
> *...trying to hound him out of office.*
> *A magazine editor claimed yesterday that he was hounded out of his job because he is a man.*
> *The campaign of hate-mail will not hound him out of his home.*

cat

3.36 **Cats** are very common and popular pets in Britain and the United States. Some people consider them to be lazy and greedy. **Cat** is used metaphorically in the expression **fat cat** to talk about people who are lazy or greedy.

If someone refers to successful business people as **fat cats**, they disapprove of them because they think that they are making too much profit for themselves, and not giving enough money to their workers or to the government.

> *...a bunch of fat cats with fast cars and too many cigars.*
> *...foreign exchange fat cats making a fortune at the expense of others.*

catty

3.37 When cats fight, they are very aggressive and use their sharp teeth and claws to hurt the cat they are fighting with. This aspect of their behaviour is referred to in the adjective **catty**.

If you say that someone, especially a woman, is being **catty**, you mean that they are being unpleasant and spiteful, usually by making nasty comments to someone or by saying unkind things about them when they are not there.

His mother was catty and loud.
She said something catty.
...catty remarks.

kitten

3.38 A **kitten** is a baby cat. **Kittens** are thought to be charming and playful, and not independent or vicious in the way that adult cats can be. **Kitten** is used metaphorically to talk about women who are considered to be very sexually attractive and who flirt a lot.

Journalists sometimes refer to a very glamorous and sexually attractive young woman as a **sex kitten**, especially if they think that she deliberately behaves in a provocative way. This is often used about actresses, singers, and models.

...French sex kitten Brigitte Bardot.
Sharon Stone admits she has to fight against being typecast as a blonde sex kitten.

kittenish

3.39 If you say that a woman's behaviour is **kittenish**, you mean that she flirts with men in a playful and youthful way.

There was something kittenish about her.
She was playful, innocent and kittenish.

Farm animals

3.40 This section looks at words for animals which are commonly kept on farms in Britain and the United States.

cow

3.41 A **cow** is a large female animal that is kept for its milk. Many people think that cows are stupid and ugly. If someone calls a woman a **cow**, they dislike her because they think she is unpleasant or stupid. This is an offensive use.

I longed to say to her 'Why don't you do it yourself, you old cow?'
All I could hear was the producer screaming 'What the hell does the silly cow think she's doing?'
'I've had my eye on her. Stupid cow, she thinks I don't know what goes on.'

bull

3.42 A **bull** is a male animal of the cow family. Bulls are big and fierce, and are associated with strength, confidence, and aggression.

In economics, **bulls** are investors on the stock market who buy shares in the hope that their value will go up and they will be able to sell them at a profit. A **bull market** is a situation in which a lot of people are buying shares and values are going up.

> *The bulls are dejected. Tokyo's stockmarket never did what they hoped.*
> *Now the demand for homes is picking up. Bulls of residential property even talk of a shortage.*
> *During the bull market in property, with prices rising fast, auctions became increasingly popular.*
> *Such bids mostly happen in a bull market.*

See also **bear: 3.87**.

bullish

3.43 In economics, if the market is **bullish**, people feel optimistic about future prices, so they want to buy shares.

> *The latest survey of manufacturers shows the biggest increase in optimism for ten years. It is particularly bullish about exports.*
> *Most bankers are still bullish, at least in public.*

See also **bearish: 3.88**.

3.44 If someone is **bullish** about something, they are cheerful and optimistic about it.

> *He was bullish about the union's future.*
> *The athlete was clearly in a bullish mood.*
> *...bullish speeches on law and order and the economy.*

pig

3.45 A **pig** is a pink or black animal with short legs and not much hair on its skin. Pigs are often kept on farms for their meat. Pigs are thought to be dirty, greedy, and smelly. If you call someone a **pig**, you think they are very unpleasant, for example, because they have been greedy, rude, or unkind.

> *...a bunch of racist pigs.*
> *'What a pig you are, Joe.'*
> *He is a complete pig to the women in his life.*

3.46 Men who do not believe in women's rights and who think that men are naturally superior to women are sometimes referred to as

chauvinist pigs or **male chauvinist pigs**. This is intended as an insult.

> *Before you dismiss me as a <u>chauvinist pig</u>, I am very much in favour of equal rights.*

3.47 Pig is also used as an insult or as a joke to refer to someone who eats too much or who is very fat.

> *I was a fat slob, a <u>pig</u> hooked on cocaine.*
> *'Go on, be a <u>pig</u> and eat it all.'*

3.48 If people eat much more than is good for them on a particular occasion, especially if they eat food that is not healthy, you can say that they are **pigging themselves** or that they are **pigging out**. These expressions are informal.

> *A vicar's wife accused them of '<u>pigging themselves</u>' at the expense of churchgoers.*
> *I'm still very careful about what I eat but if I do <u>pig out</u> at the weekend or drink alcohol, I'll be careful all the following week.*
> *He <u>had</u> probably <u>pigged out</u> in a fast-food place beforehand.*

3.49 If you say that someone is **pig-headed**, you mean that they refuse to change their mind about something, even when it is obvious that they are wrong.

> *...the <u>pig-headed</u> politicians who run this country.*
> *Jane thought he was the most <u>pig-headed</u> man she'd ever met.*

swine

3.50 A **swine** is a pig. This an old-fashioned or technical word. **Swine** is used metaphorically in a similar way to **pig**. If you call someone a **swine**, you are showing your anger and disapproval because you think they have behaved extremely badly. **Swine** is used more commonly about men than about women, and is used especially to refer to violent criminals, in order to express disgust at their actions.

Note that the plural form is also **swine**.

> *He and his young family were terrified of the kidnapper. He said, 'I won't feel safe until the <u>swine</u> is behind bars.'*
> *Look at the things that have been done by these <u>swine</u>.*
> *'Tell me what you did with the money, you <u>swine</u>.'*

hog

3.51 A **hog** is a pig. **Hog** is used metaphorically to show that you think someone has behaved in a selfish or greedy way.

3.52 If someone **hogs** something, they take all of it or use it in a greedy or impolite way. This is an informal use.

Have you done hogging the bathroom?
He had to be reminded, at times, not to hog the conversation.

3.53 If you call someone a **road hog**, you think that they drive in an inconsiderate way that is dangerous to other people.

This can also be spelt **roadhog**.

They are lethal road hogs.
...a roadhog terrorised a woman driver.

sheep

3.54 A **sheep** is a farm animal with a thick woolly coat. They are kept for wool or for their meat. Sheep are considered to be very stupid, especially because if one sheep does something, the others will usually copy it, even if it is a very dangerous thing to do. If you refer to a group of people as **sheep**, you disapprove of them because you think that they do not have their own opinions but just copy what other people say or do and believe what other people tell them to believe.

'DJs are a load of miserable sheep,' he said.
We're not political sheep.

sheepish

3.55 You can say that someone looks **sheepish** if they look a little embarrassed or ashamed of themselves because they have done something silly or a little dishonest.

He said 'Give me that wallet now.' The man looked sheepish and handed it over.
Alison returned, looking sheepish.
He gave them a sheepish grin and left without further explanation.

lamb

3.56 A **lamb** is a young sheep. People sometimes use **lamb** to refer to people who they are fond of, and who are gentle and kind, and do not cause trouble. Some people use **lamb** to refer to people who they feel sorry for.

Be a lamb, will you? I'll take care of her, but come and get me in, say, ten minutes.
I'll stay with the poor little lamb just as long as he needs me.

horse

3.57 A **horse** is a large animal which people can ride, or which can be used to pull ploughs and carts. Horses are very energetic and if they are not trained properly they behave in a very wild and uncontrolled way.

If someone **horses around**, they play in a foolish way, usually with other people. **Horse around** is used especially to describe the behaviour of children and teenagers.

> *This is a research site. Not the best place for a couple of boys to be horsing around.*
> *Later that day I was horsing around with Katie when she accidentally stuck her finger in my eye.*

Note that the noun **horse** is not usually used metaphorically.

Wild animals

3.58 This section looks at words for wild animals, including both animals which live in the wild in Britain, such as **rats**, **foxes**, and **mice**, and animals which live in the wild in other countries, such as **bears** and **wolves**.

vermin

3.59 **Vermin** are animals such as rats and mice which cause problems to humans by carrying disease and destroying crops and food. You can use **vermin** to refer to people who you strongly disapprove of because you think that they are harmful and dangerous to society.

> *The vermin are the people who rob old women in the street and break into houses.*
> *The multi-cultural society is working quite well and we must not let a minority of racist vermin continue to make trouble.*

mouse

3.60 A **mouse** is small furry animal with a long tail. Mice are timid animals and will run away from noise or sudden movements. If you say that someone is a **mouse**, you think that they are extremely quiet and shy and that they are not able to disagree with other people and say what they think.

> *After that row she got up and went, most surprisingly. I always thought her a mouse.*

I didn't know how to act. I didn't want to be too aggressive but I didn't want to be a <u>mouse</u> either.

mousy

3.61 If you describe someone as **mousy**, you mean that they are quiet and rather dull.

A short, <u>mousy</u> woman, this was her first teaching job and she wasn't enjoying it.
...the <u>mousy</u> little couple from Manchester who had bored her so thoroughly.

·**3.62** If you describe someone's hair as **mousy**, you mean that it is mid-brown in colour, like the colour of a mouse's fur, and that it seems dull and unattractive to you.

He was average height, average build, with <u>mousy</u> hair and a forgettable face.

Note that this can also be spelt **mousey**.

rat

3.63 A **rat** is a furry animal with a long tail. **Rats** look rather like large mice. Rats are considered to be very unpleasant animals because they spread disease and destroy food and crops. **Rat** is used metaphorically in a similar way to words such as **pig** and **bitch**, to show that you think someone has behaved in an unacceptable way.

3.64 If you call someone a **rat**, you are angry with them or dislike them, usually because they have tried to cheat you or deceive you. **Rat** is used more commonly to talk about men than women.

He saved three people from a burning house in the Blitz, but was a thieving <u>rat</u> otherwise.
'He did a terrible thing. He's a <u>rat</u>.' Tears splashed down Clare's cheek.

3.65 If one person **rats on** another, the first person tells other people a secret or something unpleasant about the second person, in order to cause trouble. You can also say that someone **has ratted on** you if they have broken a promise to you. Both these uses express strong disapproval.

Good friends <u>don't rat on</u> each other.
If she walked out she had no guarantee that Hal <u>wouldn't rat on</u> her.
'Give us the gun,' he said, 'I <u>won't rat on</u> you.'
She claims he <u>ratted on</u> their divorce settlement.

weasel

3.66 A **weasel** is a small animal with a long thin body, a tail, short legs, and reddish-brown fur. Weasels are thought to be very clever, cunning animals. **Weasel** is used metaphorically as a verb in expressions which refer to behaviour which involves cheating or deceiving someone.

Note that the noun **weasel** is not usually used metaphorically.

3.67 If someone **weasels out** of a duty or promise, they manage to escape from doing their part of it. This expression is used showing disapproval.

> *A buyer will not usually be able to <u>weasel out</u> of these promises later.*
> *The fact that the US is saying these things makes it easier for the British Government to <u>weasel out</u>.*

3.68 You can refer to speech or writing which you think is intended to deceive or trick people as **weasel words**. This is a literary expression.

> *Advertisers use <u>weasel words</u> to appear to be making a claim for a product when in fact they are making no claim at all.*

ferret

3.69 A **ferret** is a small, fierce animal related to the weasel. Ferrets live in the wild. They are also kept by people as they can be used to hunt rabbits and rats because they can go into small burrows and tunnels. **Ferret** is used metaphorically as a verb to talk about searching or hunting for something in a hurried and intense way.

Note that the noun **ferret** is not usually used metaphorically.

3.70 If you **ferret** somewhere for something, you search busily for that thing, in an enthusiastic but not very organized way.

> *The Director General <u>ferretted</u> in his breast pocket for his reading glasses.*
> *His enthusiasm is clear as he <u>ferrets</u> for specimens.*

3.71 If someone **ferrets out** something, especially information, they find it by searching very thoroughly for it.

> *Several top American columnists <u>ferret out</u> information that others would prefer to keep confidential.*
> *O'Connor was the person who <u>ferretted out</u> the truth in this case.*

shrew

3.72 A **shrew** is a small animal with brown fur, like a mouse with a pointed nose. In former times, shrews were thought to be aggressive animals, and people used to refer to a woman as a **shrew** if she was spiteful, aggressive, or bad-tempered. This use is much less common these days, and many people consider it to be offensive to women.

The woman you describe sounds like a tyrant and a shrew.
He announced that his step-mother was a shrew and he had no intention of going there again.

shrewish

3.73 If you describe a woman as **shrewish**, you mean that she is spiteful, aggressive, and bad-tempered. This is an old-fashioned word.

She was in her mid-forties, unmarried, shrewish and immensely proud of her efficiency.
...a shrewish look.

hare

3.74 A **hare** is an animal like a large rabbit with very long ears. Hares can run very quickly, and are often thought to behave in a mad or uncontrolled way. **Hare** is used metaphorically as a verb to talk about moving very quickly in a slightly panicky way.

Note that the noun **hare** is not usually used metaphorically.

3.75 If you say that someone **hares off** somewhere or **hares** there, you mean that they go there as quickly as possible, in a great hurry. This is used in informal English, and is often used to show that you think someone is hurrying in a silly or unnecessary way.

He hared off towards the main gate, shouting wildly to the guard house to raise the alarm.
...an over-protective mother who keeps haring off to ring the babysitter.
He went haring round to her flat.

3.76 A **hare-brained** idea or plan is foolish and not likely to succeed.

This isn't the first hare-brained scheme he's had.

squirrel

3.77 A **squirrel** is a small furry animal with a long bushy tail and long sharp teeth. Squirrels live in trees, and they eat nuts and berries.

In summer and autumn, squirrels bury supplies of nuts and berries so that they can dig them up and eat them in the winter. **Squirrel** is used metaphorically as a verb to talk about hiding or storing things secretly.

If someone **squirrels away** something such as money or food, they save it carefully, often in a secret place, so that they can use it later.

> *Japan's savings rate is too high as consumers squirrel away huge sums for the downpayment on a home.*
> *She must have had a second bottle squirrelled away.*

fox

3.78 A **fox** is an animal which looks rather like a dog and which has reddish-brown fur and a long bushy tail. Foxes are thought to be very clever, and many people do not like them because they spread diseases and sometimes kill farm animals. **Fox** is used metaphorically to talk about clever or cunning behaviour.

3.79 If you call someone a **fox**, you mean that they are clever, but that they often do things in a deceitful or secretive way.

> *'You sly fox,' I said. 'I get your message.'*
> *Enrico was too good, an old fox, cunning. He was giving nothing away.*

3.80 If something **foxes** you, it is so difficult or clever that you cannot understand it. If you **are foxed**, you are puzzled and do not know what to do next.

> *Motorists have always been quick to devise ways of foxing the system.*
> *This is the sort of proposal that foxes the opposition.*
> *Our accident investigation experts are going to be completely foxed by this one.*

foxy

3.81 If you describe someone as **foxy**, you mean that they are clever in a deceitful, secretive way.

> *...a quick, cunning, foxy child.*
> *He had wary, foxy eyes.*

3.82 If a man describes a woman as **foxy**, he means that he finds her sexually attractive. This use is most common in informal American English.

> *I saw you on TV. I said to my agent, that is one foxy lady.*

wolf

3.83 A **wolf** is a wild animal that looks like a large dog. Wolves are very fierce animals which survive by hunting and killing other animals. **Wolf** is used metaphorically to talk about greedy or threatening behaviour.

3.84 If someone **wolfs** their food, or **wolfs** it **down**, they eat extremely quickly, so that they do not have time to chew or taste their food properly.

> *As I gratefully <u>wolfed down</u> the food I realised that I had not eaten anything hot and substantial since my last dinner in Llasa.*
> *The salad appeared in a bowl with some dressing and I <u>wolfed</u> it down.*
> *They had eaten standing up, <u>wolfing</u> the cold food from dirty tin plates.*

3.85 If you say that someone is a **lone wolf**, you mean that although they are part of a group, they do not join in with what all the other people in the group do as they prefer to be alone or to work alone. **Lone wolf** is often used in this way to suggest that someone is dangerous or a threat to the group, as it is difficult to know how they are likely to behave in a particular situation.

> *Chervin, among his peers, is something of a <u>lone wolf</u>.*

wolfish

8.86 If you describe a man or his behaviour as **wolfish**, you mean that he behaves in a way that seems sinister or threatening. This is a literary use.

> *He began his speech with a <u>wolfish</u> grin.*
> *He was handsome enough, in a <u>wolfish</u> kind of way.*

bear

3.87 A **bear** is a large, strong animal with thick fur and sharp claws. Bears are not fierce, but they will fight and kill people if they think that they are threatening them or their young. Bears are associated with defensive behaviour.

In economics, **bears** are investors in the stock market who sell shares with the intention of buying them back when their prices have fallen. In a **bear market**, prices are falling because a lot of people are uncertain about the future, and so are more likely to sell than to buy.

> *Even the <u>bears</u> on Wall Street agree that the company's operating profits will improve.*
> *The Dow had dropped sixty-three points the previous Monday and the <u>bears</u> would expect another drop.*

Wait two or three years for the next <u>bear market</u>, and buy into the company.

See also **bull: 3.42**.

bearish

3.88 In economics, if the market is **bearish**, people are uncertain about future prices, so they are more likely to sell shares than to buy them.

Women were especially <u>bearish</u>, fewer than a quarter of them expected share prices to <u>go up</u>.
Japanese banks and life insurers remain <u>bearish</u> .

See also **bullish: 3.43**.

ape

3.89 Apes are chimpanzees, gorillas, and other animals in the same family. Apes are the animals most similar to humans. When apes are kept in activity, they often try to copy actions that they see people do. This idea of copying someone's behaviour in a rather clumsy way is used in the verb **ape**.
Note that the noun **ape** is not usually used metaphorically.

3.90 If someone **apes** something or someone, they try to behave like them. People often use **ape** with this meaning to show that they think the imitation is amusing or inferior.

He <u>apes</u> their walk and mannerisms behind their backs with hilarious results.
We should not attempt to <u>ape</u> the past but to bring the best of the past out into the present.
The best British music isn't necessarily made with huge budgets or by <u>aping</u> the latest trends from across the Atlantic.

3.91 If someone **goes ape**, they behave in an uncontrolled fashion because they are very excited or annoyed about something. This is an informal expression.

The crowd <u>went ape</u>.
He is sure as hell <u>going to go ape</u> that you didn't see Rocky yesterday.

monkey

3.92 A **monkey** is an animal with a long tail. Monkeys live in trees in hot countries, and belong to the same family as gorillas and chimpanzees. Monkeys are thought to be very mischievous, and people sometimes call a naughty child a **cheeky monkey** or a **little monkey**.

She's such a little monkey.

3.93 If someone **monkeys around**, or **monkeys with** something, they play with it or interfere with it in an irresponsible way. This expression is used showing disapproval.

Genetic engineering must stop short of monkeying around irresponsibly with the species.
Not a day goes by without him getting in and monkeying with something.

tigerish

3.94 A **tiger** is large member of the cat family which lives in the wild in parts of Asia. Tigers have orange fur with black stripes, and are fierce animals. This idea of being fierce and determined is used in the adjective **tigerish**.

If you say that someone is **tigerish**, you mean that they are brave and aggressive in a way that you admire, and that they seem determined to make the best of any situation.

He's the least naturally talented of the four of us but for mental toughness he's as tigerish as any of us and sometimes more so.
His brain works so quickly that he's always one step ahead of even the most tigerish opponents.
...tigerish determination.

The noun **tiger** is not usually used metaphorically, except in poetic or literary writing.

dinosaur

3.95 **Dinosaurs** were large reptiles that lived on the earth and then became extinct millions of years ago. **Dinosaur** is used metaphorically to refer to something which is no longer considered to be useful or valuable.

If you say that a person, system, or machine is a **dinosaur**, you think that they are very old-fashioned, and should be replaced by a new person, system, or machine that is more modern.

'You're a dinosaur,' Michael said. 'The world has moved on and you don't even know it.'
True, more judges are now being appointed in their late forties and early fifties, but many courts are still presided over by dinosaurs in their late sixties and early seventies.
As an international venue it's a bit of a dinosaur.

4 Buildings and Construction

4.1 This chapter looks at words used to talk about homes and buildings. It begins by looking at words for construction and building, such as **build** and **demolish**. Then, words for buildings and parts of buildings, such as **foundation**, **wall**, and **roof**, are discussed, and finally words for entrances, such as **door**, **gateway**, and **window**.

Construction and building

4.2 Many of the words for building and construction are used to talk about creating and strengthening relationships and businesses.

build

4.3 To **build** something such as a house or a wall means to make it by joining things together. **Build** is used metaphorically to talk about creating and developing things.

4.4 If you **build** something such as a relationship or a career, you start it and gradually make it stronger until it is successful.

Since then the two have built a solid relationship.
I also tried to build an atmosphere of co-operation by asking what we could do to boost the business.
Government grants have enabled a number of the top names in British sport to build a successful career.
During this time he has built a fine reputation for high standards in the field.

4.5 If you **build on** something, you use that thing as a base or starting point and go on to develop your ideas, relationship, or business from it.

It builds on the work presented at a conference in January 1989.
The second half of the chapter builds on previous discussion of change and differentiation in home ownership.
The Guardian reports that the Labour Party is building on its lead position over the Conservatives.

4.6 **Build up** is used in a similar way to **build**. If you **build** something **up**, you deliberately develop it or you allow it to develop.
This use of **build up** is often used with a positive meaning.

Ten years ago, he and a partner set up on their own and built up a successful fashion company.
The following year he borrowed enough money to buy his first hotel and spent three years building up a hotel empire.

*The self-confidence that she <u>had built up</u> so painfully was still
paper-thin; beneath it hid despair and cold anger.*
*While saving to travel abroad he also has to clear the debts he
<u>built up</u> over three years of studying.*

4.7 If something unpleasant or undesirable **builds up**, it gradually
becomes larger or more significant.

This use of **build up** never takes an object.

*His report says 10 am is the best time to ask for favours, before
stress <u>builds up</u> and people become irritable.*
*Express any resentment quickly, politely and firmly, before it
<u>builds up</u> into uncontrollable anger.*
By early afternoon queues <u>were</u> already <u>building up</u>.

construct

4.8 To **construct** something such as a building means to make it by
joining things together. **Construct** is a more formal word than **build**.
It is used metaphorically to talk about the way ideas and systems are
created and understood.

4.9 If someone **constructs** something such as an idea, a scientific
theory, or a system, they develop it by putting other ideas or thoughts
together. This is a formal use.

*The truth is that standard economic models <u>constructed</u> on the
evidence of past experience are of little use.*
*In an attempt to overcome that, the city <u>is</u> actually <u>constructing</u>
an environmental protection plan.*

4.10 If you say that an idea **is constructed** in a particular way, you
mean that it is usually interpreted and understood in that way,
although there might be other ways of interpreting or understanding
it. **Construct** is used in this way in academic writing.

*Increasingly, scientific knowledge <u>is constructed</u> by small num-
bers of specialized workers.*
*These are affected by many factors: the child's and the mother's
personalities, social circumstances, and the way motherhood <u>is</u>
<u>constructed</u> in our society.*
*Feminism must integrate the experiences of black women and
take on board an understanding of racially <u>constructed</u> gender
roles.*

demolish

4.11 To **demolish** a building means to destroy it completely. **Demolish** is used metaphorically to say that something such as an idea or an

argument has been proved wrong in a very forceful and effective way.

4.12 If you say that one person **has demolished** another person or their ideas, you mean that the first person has shown or persuaded other people that the second person is completely wrong.

In his toughest speech yet on the economy, Mr Major demolished his critics.
The newspaper published an article by its chief political columnist which demolished this argument.

4.13 If someone **demolishes** an idea, especially one that a lot of people hold, they show everybody that this idea is wrong.

McCarthy demolishes the romantic myths of the Wild West.
David is keen to demolish preconceptions about the sign-writing business as a small-time trade done in backstreet workshops.

demolition

4.14 **Demolition** is the act or process of demolishing something.

Sports commentators sometimes talk about the **demolition of** a team or player when they are emphasizing the fact that another team or player has defeated them very easily.

Arsenal showed their worth in the demolition of their North London rivals.
...Swansea's demolition of the world champions.

cement

4.15 **Cement** is a thick, greyish paste which sets very hard when it dries. It is used by builders, for example to make floors and to make the bricks in a wall stick together. If things **are cemented** together, they are stuck together using cement, so that it would be very difficult to break them apart. The verb **cement** is used metaphorically to talk about strengthening things such as relationships and achievements.

4.16 If you say that someone **cements** a business or personal relationship, you mean that they make it stronger.

...cementing a successful business relationship.
The police team has cemented close ties with the hospital staff.
Doing things together cements friendships; most of my close friends are people I've worked with in some way or other.

4.17 If you say that someone **cements** success or an achievement, you mean that they do something extra which makes it certain that they will succeed or achieve a particular thing. This use is most common in journalism.

*It was no surprise when they <u>cemented</u> victory in the 66th minute
with another outstanding goal.*
*It was a part she knows could have won her an Oscar nomination
and <u>cemented</u> her career, but ill-health got in the way.*
In the process he <u>cemented</u> his control over the company.

Words for buildings and parts of buildings

4.18 Words such as **house** and **apartment**, and words for the rooms
within a house are not normally used metaphorically. **Home** has
several metaphorical uses, explained below.

home

4.19 Your **home** is the place where you live. People often feel more
safe and comfortable at home than they do anywhere else, and this
idea of belonging and being safe and comfortable is used metaphorically to talk about feeling secure or happy in a particular group or
situation.

4.20 If you say that something such as an institution or a political
party is a **home** for someone, you mean that they can feel comfortable
there because their ideas and way of life are accepted there, and there
are other members of that institution who think and live in the same
way.

*Germany's Green Party provided a political <u>home</u> for people who
felt their needs weren't being met by any of the traditional parties.*
*The party works on a local level as a <u>home</u> for conservative
councillors.*

4.21 If you say that you are **at home** in a particular situation, you
mean that you feel at ease and relaxed there.

*As the Fitzgeralds prospered, Rose received a thorough education
and was <u>at home</u> in the lecture halls of Boston.*
*They are the people most likely to be <u>at home</u> dealing with these
problems.*
*These people have relations and good contacts in China and feel
<u>at home</u> with the mainland's informal ways of doing business.*

4.22 **Home** is also used to refer to your mind or ideas in the
expressions below.

4.23 If something which you are already aware of but have not
thought about much **is brought home** to you, something happens
which makes you think about it again, and take it much more
seriously.

Having now seen their schooling systems, it has been brought home to me just how far we lag behind.
The risk of assassination was again brought home to Churchill and Roosevelt in January 1943 when they met at Casablanca.
It was a week of contrasts to bring home the harsh reality of life in modern-day Moscow.

4.24 If you **drive** or **hammer home** a message or idea, you present it to other people very forcefully, so that they cannot fail to understand or be aware of your point of view.

There was a huge propaganda campaign to drive home the message.
Thirty years of industrial experience drove that lesson home.
Today's march is meant to hammer home the fundamentalists' point of view.

See also **hammer: 5.49–5.51**.

back yard

4.25 A **back yard** is a small area directly outside the back of some houses that is just big enough to keep things such as dustbins and bicycles in. If you say that something is in your **back yard**, you mean that it is happening in an area in which you are personally involved or have some personal interest. **Back yard** is often used in this way to talk about an area of land that is close to you or to business concerns or interests which are important to you.

He said Europe had to clean up its back yard.
The first company on which he led the investigation was right in his back yard.

tower

4.26 A **tower** is a very tall, narrow building. Towers can stand alone or form part of a castle or a church, and are considered to be strong, safe structures. Because they are so tall, towers can often be seen from a very long way off. This idea of being strong in an obvious or noticeable way is used in the verb **tower**.

4.27 If you think that someone or something is obviously much better, more important, or more successful than other people or things like them, you can say that they **tower over** or **tower above** those other people or things.

Polls indicate that he towers above the party's other potential candidates in public fame.
In profit, production and most other things, Japan's two giants of consumer electronics tower above the rest of the industry.

The country now <u>towers over</u> its neighbours both in terms of population and wealth.

4.28 You can refer to someone who has been reliable and helpful to other people when everyone has been in a very difficult situation as a **tower of strength**.

Rosemary has been a <u>tower of strength</u>. She likes to stay in the background but she is determined.

towering

4.29 If you describe someone or something as **towering**, you are emphasizing that they are very impressive because of their importance, skill, or intensity. This is a literary use.

When **towering** is used in this way, it always occurs before a noun.

Picasso was the <u>towering</u> genius of the period.
Although dead, he remains a <u>towering</u> figure.
That these were <u>towering</u> intellectual achievements was not in doubt; however their influence was not great.

ruins

4.30 The **ruins** of a building are all that remains of it after it has been severely damaged, for example by a bomb or a fire. **Ruins** is used as a metaphor to talk about things that have been so badly damaged that they are almost completely destroyed.

4.31 The **ruins** of something such as an economic system, someone's life, or ideas are the parts that remain when it has been almost completely destroyed.

...citizens fleeing their country's economic <u>ruins</u>.
She lay back for a few moments contemplating the <u>ruins</u> of her idealism and her innocence.

4.32 If you say that something such as someone's life or a country is **in ruins**, you mean that it has been almost completely destroyed.

His career was <u>in ruins</u>.
With its economy <u>in ruins</u>, it can't afford to involve itself in military action.
Now another young woman's life is <u>in ruins</u> after an appalling attack.

Structures and parts of structures

foundation

4.33 The **foundations** of a building are the parts that are built first and which strengthen and support it. **Foundations** and **foundation** are used metaphorically to talk about the most important parts of something such as a system or plan, usually when these are the parts that were thought of or developed first.

4.34 The **foundation** or **foundations** of an idea, system, or plan are the things which support and strengthen it. **Foundations** can refer to things you have done such as advance preparation for a project. It can also refer to ideas which are very important to a project.

> *There is no painless way to get inflation down. We now have an excellent foundation on which to build.*
> *...providing a foundation for developmental planning and action.*
> *Don't be tempted to skip the first sections of your programme, because they are the foundations on which the second half will be built.*

4.35 If you say that someone **lays the foundations** for something, you mean that they make careful preparations for it in the hope that this will make it more successful or effective.

> *You can help lay the foundations for a good relationship between your children by preparing your older child in advance for the new baby.*
> *...the advances that laid the foundations for modern science.*
> *The foundations are being laid for a steady increase in oil prices over the next five years.*
> *At the same time the foundations were laid for more far-reaching changes in the future.*

4.36 If something that someone says or writes is **without foundation**, it is not based on facts that can be proved, and so it may not be true.

> *In support of the theory, she is forced to resort to statements which are entirely without foundation.*
> *Our view, he said, is that these claims are entirely without foundation.*
> *As he candidly admitted, French fears were not without foundation.*

4.37 If an event or an account of events in a book or newspaper **rocks** an organization or a belief **to** their **foundations**, that event is so shocking or upsetting that the organization or belief is severely damaged or even almost destroyed.

He's about to rock the foundations of the literary establishment with his novel.
My faith was rocked to its foundations.
Why has he not moved quickly to discredit the book which is rocking the monarchy to its foundations?

wall

4.38 A **wall** is one of the vertical sides of a building or a room. Walls hold buildings up, but they also form barriers between rooms and areas, and **wall** is used as a metaphor to talk about situations in which people have difficulties in communicating with each other because something comes between them.

4.39 You can refer to a **wall of** a particular attitude or behaviour, especially a **wall of silence**, to indicate that this attitude or behaviour prevents people from communicating or working together effectively.

Last night detectives faced a wall of silence from witnesses who were too frightened to tell what they had seen.
There is a wall of secrecy which must be removed if people's understandable anxieties are to be addressed.
He was tempted to say something, anything, that would break through that wall of indifference.
It doesn't take long to expose the wall of ignorance which neither information nor education seems able to penetrate.

Note that the plural form **walls** is not usually used in this way.

brick wall

4.40 A **brick wall** is a strong wall made of bricks. Brick walls are often used to form boundaries around areas of land, in order to stop people entering. **Brick wall** is used as a metaphor to talk about something that prevents a person or their plans from continuing in the way that they wanted to.

4.41 If you say that you, or your plans, have **met** or **come up against a brick wall**, you mean that other people disagree with you or are refusing to listen to your requests, so that you cannot continue with your plans. You use this expression when you think that the other people are behaving unreasonably.

When I tried for a jobshare I met a brick wall, but I persevered. I want to have time for the children.
Her applications were met by a brick wall of excuses.
I had been working hard for a long time and I felt that I'd come up against a brick wall.

4.42 If you say that you **are talking to a brick wall**, you mean that the people you are talking to refuse to listen to you or take notice of you.

> *He was absolutely right. Unfortunately, he was talking to a brick wall.*

roof

4.43 The **roof** of a building is the covering on top of it that protects the people and things inside from the weather. **Roof** is used in the expressions **go through the roof** and **hit the roof** to talk about something that exceeds a normal amount or an acceptable limit in a sudden or unexpected way.

4.44 If you say that something such as a rate or an amount **goes through the roof**, you mean that it increases or develops very quickly in an uncontrolled way. This metaphor is usually used with a negative meaning, for example to describe price increases, but it can also be used in a positive way.

> *They're the people who have seen their business rates go through the roof.*
> *The world's population is going through the roof.*
> *In recent years, the rewards have gone through the roof.*
> *How does she deal with relationships now that her career has gone through the roof?*

See also **12.22–12.28**.

4.45 If you say that someone **hits the roof** or **goes through the roof**, you mean that they suddenly become extremely angry, often in a way that you think is unreasonable or unacceptable. These expressions are informal.

> *I can remember asking my mother and she nearly hit the roof.*
> *Graham hit the roof after reading the manuscript of her autobiography.*
> *There was no explanation of what might be wrong. I went through the roof and slammed down the phone.*

ceiling

4.46 The **ceiling** of a room is the horizontal surface that forms the top part of the inside of it. **Ceiling** is used metaphorically in a similar way to **roof**, to talk about a limit on something.

A **ceiling** on something such as prices or wages is an official upper limit that has been put on it and that cannot be exceeded. This use is most common in journalism.

> *They decided to put a ceiling on the income of party leaders.*

The document proposes an income tax ceiling of fifty per cent.

Entrances

4.47 Many of the words used to describe physical entrances are also used to describe people gaining access to systems such as organizations, to having happy relationships, or to being happy or successful in other ways. In most cases these words are used with positive associations.

gateway

4.48 A **gateway** is an entrance where there is a gate which you have to pass through to get into a particular area of land. If you say that one thing is the **gateway** to another, you mean that you can understand or have access to the second thing by understanding, having, or using the first thing.

The face is the gateway to your personality.
The prestigious title offered a gateway to success in the highly competitive world of modelling.
What starts out as looking like a humiliating defeat turns out to be the gateway to a victorious and more fulfilling life.

door

4.49 A **door** is a movable piece of glass, wood, or metal which is used to open or close the entrance to a building, room, cupboard, or vehicle. Like **gateway**, when **door** is used metaphorically, it is associated with having access to things such as organizations or opportunities.

4.50 If you say that someone has **closed**, **shut**, or **slammed the door** on a possibility or an idea, you mean that they have decided not to consider it, or have behaved in such a way that it is no longer possible.

Don't let past mistakes close the door to opportunity.
His actions had shut the door on the possibility of talks.
It is one-sided, closing the door on all other teachings.
It is an instinct in time of economic difficulty to slam the door on the free trade that has brought prosperity.

4.51 If you **close** or **shut the door on** part of your life, you decide that it is completely finished, and concentrate on the future.

She is not closing the door on the marriage completely.
I don't feel like I have just closed the door on my past.

4.52 If you say that something **opens doors** for you, you mean that it gives you opportunities to do new things or to think in a different way.

The Turks have opened more doors to women than outsiders realise; nearly 20% of their lawyers are women, lots of their engineers and probably more of their university teachers than in Britain.

The reputation that he had gained would open doors for him.

Greater publicity has opened doors to understanding and acceptance.

back door

4.53 The **back door** of a building such as a house is an entrance that is situated at the back of it, and which is only usually used to go into the garden, rather than to enter or leave the house. **Back door** is used as a metaphor to refer to an unusual and unconventional way of entering something such as an institution or of introducing a rule or law.

4.54 If you say that someone has entered a university or got a job **through the back door**, you mean that they did not follow the usual entrance procedures. You may also be suggesting that this was unfair.

Shirley came into the profession through the back door 25 years ago.

If I get into Oxford University, it shouldn't be through some special back door opened to me because of my colour but because of merit.

4.55 If you say that a new law or system is being introduced **by the back door**, you mean that it is not being voted for or discussed officially, but that people are trying to introduce it quietly, without publicity or discussion. This expression is used showing disapproval.

They claim the government is privatising dentistry by the back door.

Unless there are tough controls on the use of licences, the result could be the introduction of identity cards by the back door.

4.56 If you say that a person or organization is trying to do something **through** or **by the back door**, you mean that they are trying to do that thing without being noticed, because other people might try to stop them if they knew about it.

The word is that the bank is already financing it by the back door.

key

4.57 A **key** is a specially shaped piece of metal that you put in a lock and turn in order to open or lock something such as a door or a suitcase, or to start or stop the engine of a vehicle. If you do not have the key for a particular door, suitcase, or vehicle, you cannot open it or use it. **Key** is used as a metaphor to talk about things that are very important, for example because they allow you to do, achieve, or understand a particular thing.

4.58 If you say that one thing is **the key to** another, you mean that it is very important to do or have the first thing in order to achieve the second. For example, if you say that money is **the key to** success, you mean that money is the most important factor in becoming successful, and that people cannot become successful without money.

Information was the key to success .
The truth is that dishonesty is the key to a happy relationship, says a US psychiatrist.
Planning and prioritising are the keys to service improvement.
A gentle approach is the key to maintaining beautiful, healthy-looking skin.

4.59 If you say that one thing is the **key to** another thing which is difficult to understand, you mean that it is necessary to know the first thing in order to understand the second.

It is possible to use these pictures as keys to the unconscious.
These considerations provide the key to understanding what is otherwise a complete mystery.
He had been working his way around the question which held the key to this entire affair, the question of motive.

See also **unlock: 4.69**.

4.60 The **key** question, idea, or person in an issue or problem is an extremely important one, or the most important one, which it is necessary to understand and deal with.

Chapter eight examines a number of key arguments about the social and political impact of rising levels of home ownership.
Inevitably the key issue is money.
Normality is the key word. Don't give your child the impression that something strange has happened.
Women's labour also plays a key role in the international movement of capital.

Here are some examples of words commonly used after **key** in this way:

area	feature	point
aspect	figure	post
component	issue	problem
decision	member	question
difference	part	role
element	person	sector
factor	player	word

lock

4.61 If you **lock** something such as a door, a room, or a container that has a lock, you close it securely using a key. If you **are locked in** a room, you cannot get out of it because the door has been locked and you do not have a key. If you **are locked out** of a room or a house, you cannot get in to it because the door has been locked and you do not have a key. This idea of a situation that cannot be changed is used metaphorically in **lock in** and **lock out**.

4.62 If you say that someone **is locked in** particular negative feelings, you mean that those feelings dominate their thoughts and stop them from being happy, so that it seems as if there is nothing they can do to make things better.

He was now locked in loneliness.
...unhappily married husbands and wives who are locked in misery.
So many people remain locked in the past by continually reliving the events that caused them pain.

4.63 If people **are locked in** an argument or struggle, they have been arguing with each other for a long time and it looks as if they will continue to argue.

The two communities have been locked in a bitter argument over access to building land.
His wife was locked in a continual battle with her jealous and possessive mother.
...locked in their endless struggle with each other.

4.64 If you **are locked in** conversation with someone, you are involved in a deep conversation, which it is difficult for other people to interrupt.

One Christmas he spent the entire dinner with his back to me, locked in conversation with an attractive friend of his sister.
She was locked in legal talks on the matter.

4.65 If you say that someone **is locked out of** an opportunity, you mean that they are unable to take advantage of this opportunity because of their personal situation or because other people prevent them from doing so.

The well-educated get jobs that provide them with more training while the uneducated are locked out of opportunities to improve their skills.
I feel locked out of life's larger possibilities.
After taking part in a strike to better low-paid teachers' conditions she found herself locked out of employment.

4.66 If you say that someone's eyes **lock on** something, you mean that the person sees that thing and keeps their eyes fixed on it.

She shook her head. 'No. I'll be fine,' she said, and as her eyes locked on mine she added 'I'll still be here when you get back.'
He stepped away from the body and began pacing about, his eyes locked on the ground.

unlock

4.67 If you **unlock** something such as a door, a room, or a container that has a lock, you open it using a key. **Unlock** is used as a metaphor to talk about beginning to understand something which you used to find difficult or mysterious, or which was kept secret.

4.68 If you **unlock** something that has been mysterious, hidden, or secret before, or that has not been used before, you find a way to understand it or to use it.

So we have an opportunity now to really unlock the secrets of the universe in ways that have not been available to us before.
I like the Surrealist movement, they were keen on unlocking the mind and understanding it.

4.69 If you say that one thing is the **key to unlocking** or the **key** that **will unlock** another thing, you mean that the first thing is necessary to understand or use the second.

Education and training is the key that will unlock our nation's potential.
By replacing hypnosis with free association, Freud found the key that unlocked his system. By 1896 he had named it psychoanalysis.
For many it is the key to opening dark corners of the mind, for others it unlocks unused muscles.

window

4.70 A **window** is a space in the wall of a building or in the side of a vehicle which is covered in glass so that it lets light in and so that you can see out. **Window** is used as a metaphor to talk about something that helps you to understand a particular situation or subject.

If you have a **window on** something, you have an opportunity to see it in a new way or to get a new understanding of it.

The event at York University offers a window on the latest green technology.
They were vital, unforgettable matches that gave us a new window on the game.

5 Machines, Vehicles, and Tools

5.1 Many of the words used to talk about **machines** and parts of machines are also used metaphorically. Words such as **machinery** and **mechanism** are used to refer to institutions and systems which operate on a large scale. Words for parts of machines are often used to refer to the technical details of these systems. Some of the verbs used to describe the ways that machines work are also used metaphorically.

These metaphors are frequently used when talking or writing about governments, law, or economics.

This chapter begins with words for machines, such as **machinery** and **mechanism**, and for parts of machines and mechanical processes, such as **wheel** and **pump**. Next it looks at words for tools and working with tools, such as **hammer** and **grind**. Finally, words for vehicles and parts of vehicles, such as **vehicle** and **gear**, are discussed.

Machines

machinery

5.2 Machinery is used to refer to machines in general, or to machines that are used in a factory or on a farm. **Machinery** is used metaphorically to refer to systems or processes that deal with a particular thing in a methodical or complex way.

5.3 You can refer to **the machinery of** the law or **the legal machinery** to talk about the way the law operates, especially when you think that it is rather slow and complicated, or when you are thinking of it as an impersonal system.

> *They affirmed their faith in the League of Nations and <u>the machinery of international law</u>.*
> *The authorities now seem to be finally setting in motion <u>the legal machinery</u> to try and sentence those it regards as responsible for a counter-revolutionary rebellion.*

5.4 Machinery is also used to refer to details and procedures of governments and economic systems.

When **machinery** is used in this way, it must occur after an adjective or before a noun in the structure '**the machinery of** something'.

> *<u>The machinery of</u> democracy could be created quickly but its spirit was just as important.*
> *Five years of tinkering with <u>the machinery of</u> the socialist economic system has left the people worse off than they were.*

It revealed the well-oiled machinery of a party that has been in power since 1948.

mechanics

5.5 Mechanics is the study of natural forces such as gravity that act on moving or stationary objects. **Mechanics** is used as a metaphor in a similar way to **machinery**, to talk about the details and procedures of complicated systems such as the law, government, and economics. **Mechanics** is often used to emphasize that you are talking about the practical aspects of something rather than the general principles behind it.

When **mechanics** is used in this way, it is always used in the structure 'the **mechanics of** something'.

The National party are edging towards agreement on the timing and mechanics of an election.
...those currently controlling the mechanics of power.
You could ask your daughter to sit down with you and run through the mechanics of organizing your accounts.

5.6 You can also talk about **the mechanics of** a process when you are referring to the technical aspects of it rather than the parts which involve your intelligence and feelings.

The one thing she didn't have to do was find a house; that came with her husband's job. But the mechanics of running a family and home changed fundamentally.
...the mechanics of Shakespeare's dialogue.
They enroll in a course that includes the mechanics of language.

mechanism

5.7 In a machine or a piece of equipment, a **mechanism** is a part, often consisting of smaller parts, which performs a particular function. **Mechanism** is used as a metaphor to talk about a procedure within a larger system which allows a particular thing to take place. It is usually used about useful or beneficial changes and events, but it can be used about things you do not like.

In cases like this, the army can by-pass the appeals mechanism altogether.
This would establish a mechanism by which they can claim financial compensation.
It is also urgent to create mechanisms for the exchange of information.

mechanical

5.8 A **mechanical** device has parts that move when it is working, often using power from an engine or electricity. **Mechanical** is used metaphorically to describe actions or responses that seem to be done just because they are expected or normal.

If you describe someone's behaviour as **mechanical**, you mean that their behaviour seems to be controlled by practical considerations and conventions rather than emotions, and that they do not seem to think about what they are doing.

...a very pretty girl at a desk giving him a mechanical smile.
Literacy teachers shouldn't be too mechanical in their approach.
I'd been trained to think my whole job was doing things to people in a mechanical way to make them better, to save their lives. This is how a doctor's success is defined.

mechanically

5.9 If you do something **mechanically**, you do it because you feel you are expected to do it, or because it is a habit, and you do not really think about it.

He nodded mechanically.
I dressed mechanically, phoned his office, and notified close relatives and the children that he was dead.

Parts of machines

workings

5.10 The **workings** of a piece of equipment are the moving parts that make it work. **Workings** is used metaphorically in a similar way to **machinery** and **mechanics** to refer to the way a system or process works.

5.11 The **workings** of a society, organization, or system is the way the people or processes involved in it function. **Workings** is often used in this way to suggest that it is not easy to understand how this society, organization, or system functions if you are not involved in it.

The congress approved some modest changes, intended to make the party more democratic in its workings.
Public services are essential to the workings of private production and distribution.
...the workings of the free market.

5.12 You can refer to the way someone thinks and makes decisions as **the workings of** their **mind**.

> *How could any man ever understand <u>the workings of</u> a woman's <u>mind</u>?*
> *<u>The workings of</u> the human <u>mind</u> are subtle and little known.*

clockwork

5.13 A **clockwork** toy or device has machinery inside it so that it works if it is wound up with a key. **Clockwork** devices are very reliable and work in a very regular way, and **clockwork** is used metaphorically to talk about things that happen in a reliable or regular way.

If you say that something such as a plan or arrangement works **like clockwork**, you mean that it happens in exactly the way it was planned, without any problems. You can also say that something happens with **clockwork** regularity or efficiency to mean that it happens very regularly or efficiently.

> *He soon had the household running <u>like clockwork</u>.*
> *The journey there went <u>like clockwork</u>; flying out from Gatwick it took seven hours, door to door.*
> *Each day a howling wind springs up from the south with almost <u>clockwork</u> regularity.*

engine

5.14 The **engine** of a car or other vehicle is the part that produces the power which makes the vehicle move. This idea of having the power to make something work is used to talk about actions, events, or situations which can make other things happen or change.

If you describe something as, for example, an **engine** for change or an **engine** for improvement, you mean that it is a very powerful force which changes or improves things within society, the economy, or the government. This use is most common in journalism.

> *The private sector is also an <u>engine</u> of innovation.*
> *Adapting foreign technology can no longer serve as a main <u>engine</u> of growth.*
> *The worst affected areas will be small businesses, the main <u>engine</u> of job-creation.*

engineer

5.15 When a vehicle, bridge, or building **is engineered**, it is constructed or built using scientific methods. The verb **engineer** is used metaphorically to say that something has been arranged or created in a deliberate and clever way.

If you say that someone **engineered** a situation or a change, you mean that they deliberately caused it to happen, in a clever and indirect way, usually in order to gain an advantage for themselves. This is usually used showing disapproval.

> *As far as I can remember, most of our early arguments <u>were engineered</u> by her simply because she felt like a fight and enjoyed one.*
> *He <u>had engineered</u> the trip, partly, at least, to escape from emotional unhappiness at home.*
> *They have repeatedly accused them of <u>engineering</u> the violence in the townships.*

tick over

5.16 If an engine **is ticking over**, it is working at a low speed or rate, for example because it is not being used fully. This idea of operating more slowly than usual and not producing very much is used as a metaphor to talk about businesses and organizations which do not seem to be working very effectively.

5.17 If you say that a business, organization, or country **is ticking over**, you mean that it is continuing to function, but it is not expanding or producing very much, possibly because people are waiting for changes to happen.

> *The project might be kept <u>ticking over</u> indefinitely.*
> *The president's decision will keep the government <u>ticking over</u> until next Thursday.*

5.18 If you say that your mind **is ticking over**, you mean that you are continuing to think about something, mainly in order to keep your mind active.

> *A business would be a good thing for us. It would keep the brain <u>ticking over</u>.*
> *The coffee was perfect and by the time I was halfway through my first cup my brain <u>was ticking over</u> much more briskly.*

wheel

5.19 In a large machine or engine, a **wheel** is a circular object which turns in order to make another part of the machine move.

The **wheels** of a system are the parts of it which work together to keep the whole system functioning. **Wheels** is almost always used with another metaphor related to machines, such as **oil** or **grind**.

5.20 To **oil the wheels** of a system means to do something to help it to work more efficiently. This use is most common in journalism.

> *The media are important to a healthy, well-functioning economy; they are a commercial activity that <u>oils the wheels</u> of the economy.*

...keeping the wheels of business oiled.

5.21 To **grease the wheels** of a system means the same as to **oil** them. This use is most common in journalism.

Money-supply growth is currently inadequate to grease the wheels of recovery.
They greased the wheels of the consumer boom by allowing us to buy what we want, when we want.

5.22 If you say that the **wheels** of a system **grind** slowly, or **are grinding**, you mean that the system is working, but apparently with difficulty, because it is inefficient, or because there are many obstacles.

The wheels of justice grind slowly, and it wasn't until eight years later that 13 people were convicted.
...the grinding wheels of historical change.

5.23 To set or to put **the wheels in motion** means to begin a complicated process within a system.

Mr Major has set the wheels in motion. Now let's get on with it.
It's time everyone else started believing it and put the wheels of change into motion.

5.24 To **keep the wheels turning** means to prevent a process from stopping.

If, however, it turns out that a lot more money is going to be needed to keep the wheels turning in eastern Germany, then another round of interest rate rises is expected.
...practical solutions which would keep the business wheels turning.
For decades it was these people who kept the wheels of the British economy turning.

5.25 The expression **wheels within wheels** is used to refer to a situation in which there are a number of different interests and factors, so that it is difficult to understand or to predict exactly what may happen.

There are wheels within wheels. Behind the actor's apparent freedom as a director or a producer may lie the interest of the studio subsidising the film.
Like other small isolated communities shut away from the rest of the world, there were wheels within wheels.

cogs

5.26 A **cog** is a wheel with square or triangular teeth around the edge, which is used in a machine to turn another wheel or part. **Cog** is used metaphorically to refer to part of a system that seems very small and does not seem important, but which is necessary. It is normally used with another metaphor related to machines such as **machine** or **wheel**.

If you say that something is **a cog in** a particular **machine**, you mean that it is a small part of a bigger system. **Cog** is often used in this way to suggest that the thing you are referring to is treated as if it were unimportant or insignificant.

As cogs in the Soviet military machine, the three countries' armies used to sit mainly near their western borders.
They were small, totally insignificant cogs in the great wheel of the war.
...the great advertising machine in which they were tiny cogs.

chain

5.27 A **chain** consists of metal rings joined together in a line. There are two main metaphorical uses of **chain**, based on different ideas connected to the literal meaning of the word. The first set of uses, explained at **5.28–5.32**, is related to the way chains consist of linked pieces of metal; the second set of uses, explained at **5.33–5.35**, is related to the way chains can be used to imprison people.

5.28 A **chain of** events or relationships is a series of them, that happen after or next to each other and that are connected to each other, so that each one causes or influences the one after it or nearest to it.

The murder began the chain of events that led to the fall of the government.
This discovery sets off a whole chain of reactions in the working class community.
The chain of relationships did not end there, because Lou was married to Ted, who had once been engaged to Nora before she married Arthur.

5.29 If one event starts off a **chain reaction**, it causes a large number of other, similar, events to happen in an uncontrolled way.

The authorities have so far managed to prevent a chain reaction.
We are witnessing an unstoppable chain reaction of job losses.

5.30 The **chain of command** within an organization is a connection between the people who have responsibilities, from the least senior person to the most senior, where the organization is structured so that each person is responsible to the person immediately above them.

If the officer won't help, follow the lending department's chain of command all the way to the board of directors.

With the chains of command breaking down and supplies no longer reaching their destinations, the republics and regions have begun to put their own interests first.

5.31 A **food chain** is a series of living things which are considered to be linked because each one eats the thing below it in the series.

Man, at the top end of several food chains, eats both green plants and animals.

5.32 A **chain** of shops or offices is a number of them in different places, which are all controlled or owned by a central organization. **Chain** can also be used to refer to a large company which has shops or offices in different places.

Hotel chains have made major investments in countries like Mexico and Cuba.
By the time he was forty, he had a worldwide chain of offices.
The chain plans to add at least one hundred new centers a year.

See also **link: 5.36–5.39**.

5.33 When writers or journalists are referring to politics, they sometimes talk about the **chains of** dependency or the **chains of** oppression to refer to the way people or countries have been exploited over a long period of time.

This offers the country the chance to break the chains of dependency and pursue a path of development.
...when Africa resumes her rightful place in the world and throws off the chains of oppression and exploitation.
They called on the workers of the Warsaw Pact to cast aside the chains of communism.

5.34 You can talk about the **chains of** a job, or of a way of thinking, to refer to the way that this limits what you are able to do.

It would release me from the chains of an office-based job and give me the freedom to pursue other projects, or even to travel.
That's why it was really important for me to shake off all these chains of expectations.

5.35 If someone **is chained to** something, they cannot get away from this thing, and they are unhappy in this situation because they have very little freedom.

In the bad old days women used to be chained to unhappy marriages for financial or social reasons.
He was chained to a system of boring meetings and memos.
It was incomprehensible that he would want to be chained to a job that promised neither challenge nor a chance for advancement.

link

5.36 A **link** is one of the pieces in a **chain**. **Link** has a number of metaphorical uses associated with connections and related to the uses of **chain** explained at **5.28–5.32**.

5.37 You can refer to one person or thing that forms part of a series of people or things which are connected as a **link in** a particular **chain**.

> *That action thus became an important link in the chain of events that led up to the outbreak of the First World War.*
> *The resistance forces always operated that way during the war; the various links in the chain only knew as much as it was necessary for them to know.*
> *Ultraviolet light might, by killing plankton, have removed a vital link in the ocean's food chains.*

5.38 The **weak link** in a connected series of people or things is the person or thing that you think is most likely to fail, and so destroy or weaken the rest of the system. When **link** is used in this way, it often occurs with **chain**.

> *The weakest link in the chain of administration was the way in which ships were armed.*
> *Prison visiting has long been regarded as one of the weak links in the security chain.*

5.39 You can use **missing link** to refer to information, events, or people which are not yet present or known about, but which would complete a series or system if they could be found or discovered. This use of **link** does not usually occur with **chain**.

> *Mr Savimbi said that this was the vital missing link in all previous peace negotiations.*
> *He has such creative thought and marvellous touch that he could just be the missing link in the English football manager's grand plan.*

pump

5.40 A **pump** is a device which is used to force liquid or gas to flow in strong regular movements in a particular direction. To **pump** a liquid or gas in a particular direction means to make it flow in that direction using a pump. The verb **pump** is often used as a metaphor for transferring or giving something, especially large amounts of money. Note that the noun **pump** is not usually used metaphorically.

5.41 If you say that a person or organization **has pumped** money **into** something, you mean that they have put a very large amount of money into it, possibly without enough care and attention. **Pump** is often used in this way to show disapproval.

They proposed to pump an extra £2 billion into the schools but much can be done to improve them at virtually no cost.
It therefore makes economic sense to upgrade the existing rail systems rather than pump money into roads.
New Department of Health figures yesterday showed more progress after the government pumped £39 million into cutting the longest waiting times.

5.42 To **pump out** something means to produce it or to supply it continuously, in large quantities. For example, if you say that music or films **are pumped out**, you are suggesting that the people producing or supplying them are not concerned about their artistic quality, but only with producing things in order to make money.

The two television channels pump out very violent material.
The newspapers, magazines and radio had been pumping out BRM propaganda which raised public expectations.
The Japanese companies have been pumping out plenty of new products.

Tools and working with tools

tool

5.43 A **tool** is any instrument or simple piece of equipment which you hold in your hands and use to do a particular type of work. For example, spades, knives, and hammers are all tools. **Tool** can be used metaphorically to refer to something such as a plan or a system that people use deliberately for a particular purpose.

The tests are a powerful tool for raising standards.
Long-term credit is a key selling tool which should be costed in the same way as other forms of sales promotion.
Use this book as a diagnostic tool to help you see when you do need outside support.

5.44 If you describe a person or group of people as the **tool of** another person or organization, you mean that they are in the power of that person or organization and are being used by them in a way which you do not like, or that they exist in order to do something that you do not like.

They despise you anyway as a tool of imperialism.
In this country the police are essentially a tool of repression.
The churches in East Germany were never simple tools of the communist party.

instrument

5.45 An **instrument** is a tool or device that is used to do a particular task, especially a scientific task. **Instrument** is used metaphorically in a similar way to **tool** to refer to something such as a plan or a system that people use for a particular purpose.

You can refer to a way of doing or achieving something as an **instrument of** that thing. This is a formal use.

The organization now likes to present itself as an enthusiastic supporter of political reform, not an instrument of repression.
Nuclear weapons had made war too devastating to be an instrument of policy.

lever

5.46 A **lever** is a long bar, one end of which is placed under a heavy object so that when you press down on the other end you can move the heavy object. **Levers** can be used to move objects that would otherwise be far too heavy. **Lever** is used metaphorically to refer to an action or plan which can be used to achieve a particular thing in an effective but forceful way, or to the use of force to persuade someone to do something.

They may use it as a bargaining lever.
The industrial planners' main lever of control has been their ability to direct cheap credit to the borrowers they favour.
That will give the Treasury a new lever to prise open foreign banking markets.

5.47 If one person **levers** another person into doing a particular thing, they use something such as an action or a threat to force the other person into doing what they want.

The teaching unions will try to lever up pay levels at individual negotiations.
By promising to contribute, they levered Margaret Thatcher's government into pledging money for an extension of the Jubilee Line.

leverage

5.48 **Leverage** is the force that is applied to an object when a lever is used. **Leverage** can be used as a metaphor to talk about something which gives you the power to make people do what you want them to, or to refer to something which you know or have which gives you this power.

They have little leverage beyond moral pressure.

The nature of the department store puts them at a disadvantage compared with more specialised retailers when it comes to exerting <u>leverage</u> over suppliers.

States may now have little <u>leverage</u> to force hospitals to hold down costs.

hammer

5.49 A **hammer** is a tool that consists of a heavy piece of metal on the end of a long handle and which is used to hit nails into a wall or a piece of wood, or to break things apart. To **hammer** something means to hit it with a hammer. The verb **hammer** is used metaphorically to talk about doing something in a very forceful, decisive, or destructive way.

5.50 If you say that one thing or person **hammers** another, you mean that the first thing or person damages the second severely in some way, or that the first thing or person attacks, criticizes, or defeats the second. This is an informal use.

High interest rates and adverse economic conditions <u>have hammered the UK market</u>.

The show <u>was hammered</u> by critics.

Many businesses are finding themselves increasingly <u>hammered</u> by new rules and regulations.

5.51 When people **hammer out** an agreement, they finally decide on it after a lot of argument and discussion.

German officials <u>have hammered out</u> a compromise which involves the Americans giving only technical assistance.

There may well be some way to go before the final details <u>have been hammered out</u>.

See also **hammer home: 4.24**.

nail

5.52 A **nail** is a thin piece of metal with one flat end and one pointed end. You hit the flat end of the nail with a hammer in order to push it into a piece of wood or a wall. If you **nail** something somewhere, you fix it there securely using a nail. The verb **nail** is used metaphorically to talk about doing something in an effective way which people will find it hard to find fault with or disagree with.

Note that the noun **nail** is not usually used metaphorically.

5.53 If you say that someone **has nailed** a criminal or someone who has done something wrong or immoral, you mean that they have found enough evidence to prove without doubt that he or she is guilty. This is an informal use.

*They did not arrest him that night. They felt that they <u>had</u>
<u>already nailed</u> him.*
I wouldn't come up here again, not until we've <u>nailed</u> this killer.

5.54 If you **nail down** something such as an arrangement that was
previously uncertain or unclear, you find out definite information
about it, and make other people agree with you about it.

The challenge for investigators is to <u>nail down</u> the details.
*If you can <u>nail down</u> a delivery time, you must then negotiate the
exact terms of installation.*

5.55 If you **nail** someone **down**, or **nail down** a point with someone,
you force them to agree to something, or to give you a definite answer,
when they have been trying to avoid doing this.

*They've been keen to <u>nail down</u> the ruling family's vague
promises about political reform.*

forge

5.56 A **forge** is a place where someone makes metal goods by heating
metal and hammering and bending it into shape. To **forge** an object
out of metal means to make it by heating the metal and hammering or
bending it into shape. The verb **forge** is used metaphorically to talk
about creating things, especially relationships.

Industry and education <u>forged</u> a strong partnership.
*Taylor has <u>forged</u> a closer relationship with his wife since the
shooting.*
*As the Socialist Party's most decisive leader, he <u>forged</u> an alliance
with the Christian Democrats.*
A new atmosphere of trust <u>must be forged</u>.

weld

5.57 To **weld** two pieces of metal means to join them together by
heating the edges and pressing them together, so that when they cool
and harden they form one piece. **Weld** is used metaphorically to talk
about joining people or organizations together in a permanent,
effective way.

If you say that someone or something **welds** two or more people or
things **together**, you mean they make the people or things more
united and understanding of each other, so that they work together
more effectively.

*The diverse ethnic groups <u>had been welded together</u> by the great
anti-fascist cause.*
*He said that Europe <u>was not</u> yet properly <u>welded together</u> by
common values.*

She has both the authority and the personality to weld the party together.

sharpen

5.58 If you **sharpen** a tool such as a knife, you make its edge very thin so that it is sharper and therefore more effective. The verb **sharpen** has several metaphorical uses, all of which are related to making something stronger or more effective.

5.59 You can say that your ways of thinking and behaving **have been sharpened** when you mean that they have become quicker or more precise.

It won't tell us exactly what's going on, but it will certainly sharpen our understanding of the general principles.
Racing on such roads, lined by massive marker posts, trees, drops, walls and houses, taught Moss precision and sharpened his fine judgement.

5.60 If your appetite **is sharpened**, something makes it stronger.

The Director General was taking breakfast at his desk, his appetite sharpened by the brisk walk over Hungerford bridge.

5.61 If someone's voice **sharpens** or **is sharpened**, it becomes quicker and more emotional, so that other people are likely to notice or pay attention to them.

'How is she?' Amy asked, anxiety sharpening her voice.

5.62 If disagreements between people or groups of people **sharpen**, or if they **are sharpened**, they become worse. This use is most common in journalism.

By 1971, however, the JDL had become a violent fringe group manipulated to sharpen tensions between Jews and blacks.

grind

5.63 To **grind** a substance such as corn means to crush it between two hard surfaces, usually using a machine, so that it becomes a powder. To **grind** something such as the blade of a knife means to rub it against something rough so that part of it rubs away and it becomes thinner and sharper. The idea of crushing something or wearing it away is used metaphorically to talk about situations which gradually make someone feel weaker.

5.64 If a situation or person **grinds** someone **down**, they make that person feel extremely tired and miserable over a long period of time.

I've never let male colleagues grind me down.
They are ground down by struggling for equality.

5.65 If an unpleasant situation **grinds**, or if it **grinds on**, it continues for a long time, making people feel very tired and miserable.

They are where the poverty grinds hardest.
The recession grinds on.

5.66 If you describe a situation as a **grind**, you mean that is unpleasant and very tiring, and continues for a long time, or happens frequently. You can refer to the unpleasant aspects of everyday life, such as hard and boring work, as the **daily grind**.

Festivals provided a much-needed break from the hard grind of daily work.
Have you ever thought of the kind of personality it takes to get through the tough grind of medical school?
Washing machines and dishwashers have certainly taken the grind out of some household chores.

grinding

5.67 You can describe a process which is extremely slow and boring, or a situation which is tiring and unpleasant, and which continues for a long time, as **grinding**.

Their grandfather had left his village a century ago in order to escape the grinding poverty.

Vehicles

5.68 A **vehicle** is a machine with an engine, such as a car or a bus, that is used to transport people or things from one place to another. Words for **vehicles** and parts of vehicles are often used metaphorically to talk about change and movement in people's lives.

vehicle

5.69 If you say that something is a **vehicle for** a purpose, or a **vehicle of** a particular thing, such as change or freedom, you mean that it is used in order to achieve that thing.

...the understanding that education and training matter, that they are crucial vehicles for individual development.
Every effort will be made to stop them using banks as vehicles for financing their subsidiaries on the cheap.

5.70 You can say that something is a **vehicle for** someone if it allows them to use their abilities or to express their views so that other people can hear or understand them.

> *The news agency is the traditional vehicle for official leadership statements.*
> *Neither of these shows is an interview show as such, merely a vehicle for their star presenters.*

5.71 A **vehicle for** ideas is the form in which they are expressed to other people, for example, a painting, a story, or a piece of music. This is a formal use.

> *Boccaccio describes his story as a convenient vehicle for his own experiences in love.*
> *An advertisement is not simply a vehicle for its message.*

gear

5.72 The **gears** in a vehicle such as a car are the different speeds the engine can operate at. **Gear** and words associated with changing gear are used metaphorically to talk about how energetic or active people are.

If you **move up a gear** or **step up a gear**, you suddenly put more effort into something, and become more active or successful. This metaphor is often used in sports reporting.

> *It was a classic tennis match. Edberg won the first two sets, Becker stepped up a gear and won the next two, then led 3-1 in the final set.*
> *Pressure from the media was clearly going to step up a gear now.*
> *As she approaches her fortieth birthday, the Princess has moved up a gear in the pace of her life.*

top gear

5.73 **Top gear** is the highest gear in a vehicle and the fastest speed at which the engine can operate. Someone or something that is in **top gear** is working as hard as they can, and is usually successful because of this.

> *The publicity machine was in top gear again yesterday as Madonna spent a day in Britain giving interviews to drum up interest in her new book.*
> *From that moment on his career went into top gear.*

neutral

5.74 If a vehicle is **in neutral**, the engine is not in any gear and so it is not possible to drive or control it. Vehicles are usually put into neutral when they are switched off, or when they are switched on but not moving.

If you say that you are **in neutral**, you mean that you are not making very much effort to do something, or are not really aware of what you are doing, because you are tired, or because you are thinking about other things.

I'm tired, my brain's in neutral.
This allows the practitioner to concentrate and work on areas that need particular attention, while holding stronger areas in neutral.

coast

5.75 If a vehicle **coasts** somewhere, it continues to move there with the engine switched off or without anyone pushing or pedalling it. **Coast** is used metaphorically to talk about doing something without any real effort.

If you **are coasting**, you are doing something easily and without any special effort, and you could probably do it a lot better if you tried to.

There was a time when Charles was coasting at school, and I should have told him to work harder.
The West Indies coasted to a comfortable victory shortly after lunch.

brake

5.76 A **brake** on a vehicle is a device which causes it to slow down or stop. You can refer to something which slows down or stops a particular process as a **brake** on that process.

The organization is keeping the brake on pay rises.
Population growth is also still cited by FAO experts as a major brake to food self-sufficiency.

5.77 If someone **puts a brake on** or **puts the brakes on** a process or an activity, they deliberately slow it down or stop it completely.

They have been trying to fight inflation through high interest rates which are designed to put a brake on economic growth.
It's up to the main arms suppliers, the major industrial nations themselves, to put the brakes on the arms race.

steer

5.78 To **steer** a vehicle means to control the direction it moves in. **Steer** is used metaphorically to talk about deliberately controlling the progress of a person, organization, or process.

5.79 If someone **steers** people towards doing something, they try to make them do that thing, but without making their influence obvious. If someone **steers** a conversation in a particular way, they control the conversation so that it goes in the way they want it to.

> *Two out of three women at the prestigious Oxford University Medical School consider surgery as a career. But consultant Jane Clarke says 80% of them are <u>steered</u> away from the profession by senior staff.*
> *In the film he keeps her from harm and <u>steers</u> her into accepting life without him.*
> *I <u>steered</u> the conversation so that we were deep in chat when we <u>pulled up</u> outside my door, making it seem the most natural thing in the world to ask her in for a drink.*

5.80 If you **steer away from** something, you avoid it.

> *They should have <u>steered away from</u> alcohol which just dehydrates you further.*
> *They decided that money should go to established orchestras, opera houses and theatres, <u>steering away from</u> the risk of new and untried work.*

5.81 If you **steer** a particular course of action, you follow that course of action, often one which is difficult to follow successfully, because there are problems, and you are tempted to do other things. This is a formal use.

> *Their international relations <u>had</u> previously <u>steered</u> a careful path between the competing interests of the two superpowers and their allies.*

5.82 If you **steer clear** of something, you deliberately try not to have any contacts or connections with it.

> *Now promoters <u>are steering clear</u> of rock acts. They are wary of paying out huge sums to the stars, and risking all on the shows being a success.*
> *The singer <u>has steered clear of</u> drugs and alcohol for the past eighteen months.*
> *Jonathan and I <u>had steered clear of</u> each other for a couple of days.*

6 Games and Sport

6.1 Many words which are used to talk about sport and games are also used metaphorically, especially to talk about other activities and to say whether or not they are being done fairly.

This chapter looks at some of the most common of these, starting with words for games generally, such as **play** and **game**, and then looking at words associated with **chess** and **card games**. Next, it looks at words for sports generally, then at words for specific sports, such as **fishing** and **hunting**, together with words for objects and actions associated with them, such as **bait**. The final part of the chapter looks at words used to talk about horse-racing and gambling, such as **neck and neck** and **gamble**.

Words used to talk about sport and games

play

6.2 If you **play** a game, you take part in it. The noun **play** is used to talk about how someone plays a game. Both the noun and the verb forms are used metaphorically to talk about human behaviour, especially to say whether that behaviour is fair and honest or not.

fair play

6.3 If you believe in **fair play**, you think that everyone should be treated fairly, and that rules should be followed carefully.

In a demonstration of its commitment to fair play, the Georgian Communist Party paper has carried without comment the political programmes of all its major rivals.
He described the circumstances of the ban as a departure from the basic principles of fair play.

play fair

6.4 If you say that someone does not **play fair**, you mean that they behave dishonestly or deceitfully, even though they may not actually have broken any rules or laws.

At the very least this should show you that banks don't play fair; they have two sets of rules. In both instances they win and you lose.
He had a reputation as a quiet and amiable man who played fair.
Play fair with us and you won't regret it.

play by the rules

6.5 If you say that a person or organization **plays by the rules**, you mean that they follow the correct procedures for doing something, rather than doing things in a way that may be easier and more successful, but which is not acceptable to other people.

You can say that someone **plays by** a particular kind of **rules** when they do things in the way that a particular group of people approve of.

The town's road safety officer spends his days ensuring that motorists play by the rules.

France is not complaining; it just wants everyone else to play by EC rules.

game

6.6 A **game** is an activity or sport usually involving skill, knowledge, or chance, in which you follow fixed rules and try to win against an opponent or to solve a puzzle. **Game** is used as a metaphor to talk about the way someone behaves in a particular situation, especially to say whether or not this is fair or honest. When **game** is used metaphorically, it often occurs with **play**.

6.7 Someone's **game**, or a particular type of **game**, is a particular way of behaving. It is not always fair or honest behaviour and it may involve risks, but it is a good way to behave in order to be successful or to gain an advantage over someone.

It was a dangerous game his friend had been playing.

I don't know what Morgan's game was. It came very close to jeopardizing his business empire.

play the game

6.8 If you can **play** a particular kind of **game**, you understand the way to do something in order to be successful or to gain an advantage in a particular situation. For example, if you know how to **play the game** in a job interview, you know how to give a very good impression of yourself. Sometimes you do not agree that this type of behaviour is right, but you do it anyway in order to please other people.

Her willingness to play the game by the usual rules of the establishment had hardly been rewarded.

Bankers don't generally expect that a customer knows how to play the game, which makes it easier for us to fight back.

'Established art galleries are very inaccessible to young artists' says Piers. 'They're in the business of making money so they've got to play the game.'

play someone's game

6.9 If you **play** a particular person's **game**, you behave in a way that that person will approve of, in order to gain advantages for yourself, even though you may not agree that it is the right way to behave.

If he is to win their financial support he must play their game.
He's angry at the moment because I won't play his game.

play games

6.10 If one person **plays games** with another, the first person is not honest with the second one and this may cause problems for the second person if they do not understand the situation.

They were just using her, playing games with her as if what she felt and what she had actually done didn't matter a bit.
I'm not going to play games with this man. I've run this office straight so far, and I'll continue to.
We don't play games. We're very straightforward.

6.11 If people **play games** or **play a game** involving their relationships with other people or their feelings, they express their feelings dishonestly, in order to make other people feel a particular emotion or behave in a particular way. For example, someone might pretend to be very unhappy in order to make other people feel sorry for them.

Where you play games to hide your true feelings, nobody ever wins.
Two people playing this game will obviously have an unhealthy relationship.

the game's up

6.12 If you say **'the game's up'**, you mean that someone's activities or secrets have been discovered. This expression is often used when criminals are caught.

It was when they mentioned his dental records. I nearly fainted then. We hadn't thought of that. I told myself, 'The game's up!'
He narrowed his eyes as the blue lights of the police car filled the cab. Sensing the game was up, he pulled over.

game plan

6.13 In sport, a team's **game plan** is the strategy they intend to use during a match or competition in order to win it. **Game plan** is used metaphorically to talk about the actions someone intends to take and the policies they intend to adopt in order to achieve a particular thing. This expression is used mainly in journalism.

Yesterday's attack on the city shows that the militants have their own game plan.

Sullivan outlined the government's <u>game plan</u> in his opening statement.

toy

6.14 A **toy** is an object that children play with, for example, a ball or a doll. People sometimes refer to objects that adults use for fun as **toys**, especially when they are talking about objects that are usually used for serious purposes, such as cars or computers.

Computers have become household <u>toys</u>.
He parked the car right next to the windows of the conference room. Perhaps he didn't want to take his eyes off his new <u>toy</u>.

6.15 If you say that you **are toying with** the idea of doing something or the notion of doing something, you are thinking about doing it but you have not made any serious plans to do it and you may change your mind.

I <u>had toyed with</u> the idea of dyeing my hair black, but decided against it.
She <u>had toyed with</u> the notion of going abroad that spring.
Viki <u>had been toying with</u> spending a year in Holland or Germany before settling down in England.

Words associated with chess

chess

6.16 **Chess** is a game for two people played on a chess board. Each player has sixteen pieces, including a king, and the aim is to try to move the pieces so that your opponent's king cannot avoid being captured. Chess is a very skilful and complicated game, and **chess** is used as a metaphor for complicated negotiations and for situations in which people try to gain advantages over each other by behaving in a cunning way.

6.17 You can refer to a situation in which people are trying to gain advantages over each other in a cunning way as a **chess game** or a **game of chess**.

The application is very much part of the long <u>chess game</u> which has been going on between the two communities since 1974.
A deadly <u>game of chess</u> is being fought on London's streets between the terrorists and the police, with the public as pawns.

Pawn often occurs with this use of **chess**. See **6.18**.

pawn

6.18 In chess, a **pawn** is one of the smallest and least valuable pieces.
Pawn is used metaphorically to talk about someone who has become
involved in a situation which they do not control, and in which they
are likely to be treated badly because they are not considered to be
important.

If you say that someone is a **pawn in** a situation, you mean that that
person is being used by other people for their own advantage, and that
the first person either does not realize this or cannot stop it
happening.

> *Sadly, the children are sometimes used as pawns in a struggle
> between hurt and angry parents.*
> *For half a century our city has been a pawn in the power games of
> others.*
> *I suppose I'm proving to myself that I'm not just a pawn in some
> financial system, I'm an independent person.*

stalemate

6.19 In chess, **stalemate** is a situation in which one of the players
cannot make a move that is permitted by the rules, so the game ends
and no one wins. **Stalemate** is used as a metaphor to talk about a
situation in which neither side in an argument or conflict can win or
in which no progress is possible.

> *There are signs that, after more than two weeks of political
> stalemate, progress is now being made towards the formation of a
> coalition government.*
> *There's been no end to the stalemate at a Scottish prison where
> inmates are holding a prison officer hostage.*

checkmate

6.20 In chess, **checkmate** is a situation in which you cannot stop
your king being captured, so you lose the game. **Checkmate** is used
metaphorically as a verb to talk about a situation in which one person
defeats another, often in a clever or cunning way.

If you say that one person **checkmates** another, you mean that the
first person puts the second person in a position in which they will be
defeated or put at a disadvantage, and there is nothing they can do to
stop this.

> *He had to find out what this girl was up to so he could checkmate
> her.*
> *He would have to checkmate the dirty tricksters at their own
> game.*

Cards and card games

6.21 **Card games** involve using a pack of cards to play games which involve one or more people. Some card games involve an element of skill, but the most important thing is luck, as you cannot control the cards you are given to use. There are a number of metaphors in which people's chances in life are talked about as if they were playing cards.

play your cards

6.22 If someone is faced with a situation in which they have to make difficult decisions and deal carefully with people, you can say that they **play** their **cards** in a particular way. For example, if they **play** their **cards right**, they deal with the situation successfully.

Soon, if she played her cards right, she would be head of the London office.
If she played her cards sensibly there was a new and decent life ahead of her.
He achieved this ambition through some of his father's old friendships and by playing his cards intelligently.

6.23 If you say that someone **has played all** their **cards**, you mean that they have tried all the possibilities open to them, without success. If you say that they **have another card to play**, you mean that there is still a possibility open to them, although they have tried several other things unsuccessfully.

I haven't played all my cards yet. We can still make a deal.
The deal provided him with another card to play.

6.24 If you say that someone **keeps** or **plays** their **cards close to** their **chest**, you mean that they do not tell other people about their ideas or plans for the future.

He keeps his cards incredibly close to his chest. We have no idea what he thinks.
The big companies were playing their cards close to their chests last night about where the money goes.

put or lay your cards on the table

6.25 In some card games, especially games which involve gambling, the players **put** or **lay** their **cards on the table** at the end of the game to see who has cards of the highest value and has therefore won the game. **Put** or **lay** your **cards on the table** is used as a metaphor to talk about a situation in which someone decides whether or not to reveal ideas, plans, or intentions which they had previously kept secret.

If someone **puts** or **lays** their **cards on the table**, they tell people all about their ideas, plans, or intentions, especially when they might have been expected to keep them secret.

> *I'm going to put my cards on the table and make you an offer.*
> *The star laid his cards on the table yesterday, claiming that hundreds of thousands of pounds of licence payers' money is being wasted.*
> *He says he needs a little more information; he wants to see a few more cards on the table.*

on the cards

6.26 Cards are also sometimes used to tell people's fortunes. A fortune teller chooses a number of cards randomly and then interprets the numbers and pictures on them in a special way in order to say what is going to happen in the future. This idea of guessing that a particular thing will happen because of other things that have happened is used in the expression **on the cards**.

If you say that a particular event is **on the cards**, you mean that there are signs that it is likely to happen in the near future.

> *Many City analysts believe a rise in interest rates is still on the cards.*
> *It's looking increasingly as though a return to more traditional teaching methods could be on the cards.*
> *Fifth round matches take place this weekend, with one or two surprises on the cards.*

show your hand

6.27 In a game of cards, your **hand** is the cards you have been dealt or which you have at a certain point in the game. In some card games, especially games which involve gambling, you **show your hand** at the end of the game to see who has cards of the highest value and has therefore won. **Show your hand** is used metaphorically in a similar way to **put** or **lay your cards on the table** to talk about a situation in which someone decides whether or not to reveal plans or intentions which they had kept secret.

If someone **shows** their **hand**, they let other people know what they plan to do, what they are thinking, or what they have, especially when they might prefer to keep this secret.

> *On domestic politics he seemed unwilling to show his hand too early.*
> *Events in Russia are now forcing the US President to show his hand.*

trump

6.28 In some card games, **trumps** is the suit which is chosen to have the highest value during a particular game. **Trumps** and **trump** are used metaphorically to talk about situations in which someone is able to be more successful than other people because they have an unexpected advantage.

6.29 If someone **comes up trumps** or **turns up trumps**, they are successful or helpful at a time when this is necessary, even though you might have thought earlier that they would not be.

> *Sylvester Stallone has come up trumps at the US box office with his new movie.*
> *Time was short but he came up trumps under pressure.*
> *At least you will discover where your true affections lie when certain people turn up trumps.*

6.30 In cards, if you **trump** someone, you beat them by playing a trump card, even though they had just played a card of a high value and it seemed likely that they would beat you. The verb **trump** is used metaphorically to talk about suddenly and unexpectedly defeating someone who looked likely to succeed.

If you **trump** someone, or **trump** something that they have done, you beat them by doing something similar but better than the thing that they have done.

> *Supermarket Tesco trumped the oil giants and slashed 8p off a gallon of petrol.*
> *The natural rainbow trout record was almost immediately trumped by a 29lb fish captured from Loch Tay.*
> *The research team did not want to be trumped so they had to publish their findings quickly.*

trump card

6.31 A **trump card** is one of the cards of the suit that has been chosen to be trumps, and which will beat any card of another suit. **Trump card** is used as a metaphor to talk about an advantage that someone has that will help them to be more successful than anyone else.

> *Low wages are the country's trump card at this stage of its economic development.*
> *The Republicans retain one trump card: Texans' traditional dislike for liberal causes.*
> *Mr Major has played a trump card that could enable him to cut income tax next Spring.*

Sport

6.32 Sport is used to refer to games such as football, tennis, and athletics in which individuals or teams compete against each other in physical activities. Names of particular sports are not usually used metaphorically, but words associated with particular sports, such as **goal** and **playing field**, often are.

6.33 In sport, the teams or individuals who are competing are supposed to behave well and treat the other competitors fairly whether they win or not. This has led to expressions such as **good sport** and **unsporting** being used to talk about how someone behaves in a difficult or competitive situation.

good sport

6.34 If you say that someone is **a good sport**, you mean that even when they have bad luck they are cheerful and friendly.

They thought you were being such a good sport about it.
He is really not in the mood to be a jolly good sport.

bad sport

6.35 If you say that someone is **a bad sport**, you mean that when they have bad luck or do not succeed in something that they are doing they are bad-tempered about it and do not cope with it well.

To be a bad sport means to risk almost certain humiliation by the lads at the pub.

unsporting

6.36 If you describe someone's behaviour as **unsporting**, you think that they are behaving unfairly or selfishly, especially in a competitive situation.

Mr Thomas said he felt bound to cut prices to remain competitive, but nevertheless thought his rival's conduct pretty unsporting.
They fined me 2,700 francs which I thought was rather unsporting of them.

sporting

6.37 If you have a **sporting chance** of succeeding in doing something, it is not likely you will succeed, but it is possible, so you think it will be worth trying.

There was a sporting chance of avoiding the traffic police.
There's no reason why you can't make it. You've got a sporting chance. I've got none.

player

6.38 A **player** is someone who takes part in a game or sport. **Player** is used metaphorically to talk about a person, organization, or country that takes part in a particular event or discussion, especially in order to say how important they are in it. This use is most common in journalism.

When **player** is used in this way, it usually occurs after an adjective or noun.

> *The Bank of Scotland is now a major player in management buyouts.*
> *America is not a party to the negotiations, yet it is a key player.*

goal

6.39 In games such as football and hockey, players attempt to win by hitting or kicking the ball into their opponent's **goal**, which is a type of large net. This is known as scoring a **goal**, and the team that scores the highest number of goals wins. **Goal** is used metaphorically to refer to something that a person or organization wants to do or achieve, usually in order to achieve another thing.

> *My goal is to get a good background on the subject so I can pass the Medical College Admission Test.*
> *The goal is to involve the parents in a plan to help their child do better in school.*
> *She dieted to within ten pounds of her goal weight.*

own goal

6.40 In games such as football and hockey, if a player scores an **own goal**, they accidentally kick or hit the ball into their own goal so that the other team scores a point. **Own goal** is used metaphorically to refer to something that someone does with the intention of improving their position, but which in fact makes their own position worse.

> *Because of the legislation I could not employ a woman. Women have made themselves unemployable. They have scored an own goal.*

goalpost

6.41 In games such as football and hockey, a **goalpost** is one of the two upright wooden posts that are connected by a crossbar and form the goal. In these games, the goalposts are in a fixed position so that both teams know exactly where to aim for and both have an equal chance of scoring goals. **Goalposts** is used metaphorically in the expression **move the goalposts** to talk about a situation in which one person or group of people behaves unfairly in order to gain an advantage over another person or group of people.

If you accuse someone of **moving the goalposts**, you mean that they have changed the rules in a situation in or an activity, especially to benefit themselves and to make the situation or activity harder for everyone else involved.

> *They seem to move the goalposts every time I meet the conditions that are required.*
> *He was always moving the goalposts so that we could never anticipate what he wanted.*

playing field

6.42 A **playing field** is a grassy area where sports such as football, hockey, or cricket are played. It is normally a smooth, level site. **Playing field** is used metaphorically in the expression **level playing field** to talk about how fair a situation is.

A **level playing field** is a situation that is fair because no one involved in it has an advantage over anyone else. This expression is used mainly in journalism.

> *American businessmen ask for a level playing field when they compete with foreign companies.*
> *One of the main objectives of the single market was to provide a level playing field where all EC member states could compete on equal terms.*

marathon

6.43 A **marathon** is a race in which the competitors run a distance of 26 miles (about 42 km). **Marathons** are one of the longest types of running race and are extremely difficult and tiring. **Marathon** is used metaphorically to refer to a task or journey which is extremely long or tiring.

When **marathon** is used in this way, it usually occurs before a noun.

> *Their scheduled two days of talks stretched into a marathon nine-hour session on the third day.*
> *...a marathon television show.*
> *She began her marathon journey from Maastricht with a bus ride to Calais, where she caught the ferry to Dover.*

skate

6.44 If you **skate**, you move about using ice-skates or roller-skates. Ice-skates and roller-skates work by using either a blade or wheels to slide quickly over a surface. **Skate** is used metaphorically in the phrasal verbs **skate over** and **skate around** to talk about avoiding an issue or failing to deal with it properly.

6.45 If you say that someone **skates over** or **skates around** an issue or a problem, you mean that they do not talk about it or think about it in detail, usually because it would be difficult or embarrassing for them to explain it properly.

She's had plenty of practice here in skating over unpleasant realities.
Most of these arguments skate over the evidence.
When pressed, he skates around the subject.

6.46 If you say that someone is **skating on thin ice**, you mean that they are doing something risky that may have unpleasant or serious consequences for them.

I had skated on thin ice on many assignments and somehow had, so far, got away with it.

sail

6.47 When a ship **sails**, it moves over the sea. **Sailing** is associated with easy, quick, smooth movement, and is used metaphorically to talk about situations in which someone seems to achieve something quickly or easily.

6.48 If you **sail through** a situation, or **sail into** a situation, you are able to cope with it very well without appearing to make very much effort.

I was younger then, I could have sailed through any job.
She was bright, learned languages quickly and sailed through her exams.

6.49 If you say that a task was not all **plain sailing**, you mean that it was not easy or straightforward.

Pregnancy was not all plain sailing, and once again there were problems.
We know it won't be plain sailing in the final because there are no easy games at this level.

Hunting and fishing

6.50 **Hunt**, **fish**, and a number of words associated with the activities of hunting or fishing are used metaphorically to talk about searching for and finding people and things.

hunt

6.51 **Hunting** is the activity of capturing and killing wild animals. The verb **hunt** is used metaphorically to talk about searching for someone or something, especially when it is very important for you to find that person or thing.

6.52 If the police are looking for a criminal who has disappeared after a crime, you can say that they **are hunting** that criminal.

Police were yesterday hunting the thieves.
A hit-and-run driver who killed a grandmother was being hunted yesterday.
Two men who left the third floor flat in Hove, East Sussex, at the time are still being hunted by police.

6.53 If you want something very much and are searching hard for it or trying hard to get it, you can say that you **are hunting** it, or **are hunting for** it.

My wife was very keen for years to get a plant called helichrysum and she hunted and hunted and eventually found it in a garden centre in Brighton.
He plans to save the money while he hunts for a job after being made redundant.
...two months of unsuccessful job hunting.

hunted

6.54 If someone has a **hunted look**, they look worried, as if they are expecting something unpleasant to happen soon.

A hunted look came into her eyes.
He had a hunted look about him, as if he expected someone to kick open the door at any minute.

fish

6.55 **Fishing** is the activity of catching and killing fish. The verb **fish** is used metaphorically to talk about trying to find or obtain something, especially in an awkward or indirect way.

6.56 If you **fish** somewhere, for example in a bag or in your pocket, you try to find something there, in an inefficient way, without looking. If you **fish** something from somewhere, you find it and take it out with some difficulty.

The lawyer looks at his cards again, fishes in his pocket, and lays his wallet on the table.
He fished a cigarette out and lit it, blowing the smoke into my face.
He fished some coins out of his pocket.

6.57 If you say that someone **is fishing for compliments**, you mean that they are trying to get other people to say nice things about them, for example, by asking certain questions, or by making negative statements about themselves and hoping that the person they are talking to will contradict them.

> *'They no longer find me attractive and are merely being polite.'*
> *Mark laughed. 'You're fishing for compliments,' he said, 'and*
> *you don't need to.'*

angling

6.58 Angling is another word for fishing, and **angling** is used metaphorically in a similar way to the verb **fish**.

If someone **is angling** for something, they are trying to get it, and they are using indirect methods rather than asking for it directly.

> *Are you angling for promotion? Finding out which type of worker*
> *you are, and how your colleagues see you, are the first steps to*
> *getting ahead at work.*
> *Officials have been angling for an early visit to Moscow by the*
> *new British Prime Minister.*
> *It sounds as if he's just angling for sympathy.*

Note that this verb is only used in this way in the '-ing' form.

bait

6.59 When people are hunting or fishing, **bait** is food that they use in order to attract the animal or fish they are trying to catch. **Bait** is used metaphorically both as a noun and a verb to talk about something that is used to try to persuade someone to do a particular thing.

6.60 If one person offers another person something in order to persuade them to do something, usually something that they would not usually want to do or that it would be wrong for them to do, you can refer to the thing that is offered as **bait**.

> *Gary Mason was last night warned not to accept former world*
> *heavyweight champion George Foreman's bait of a £230,000 offer*
> *to fight again.*

6.61 If one person **baits** another, the first person deliberately tries to make the second person angry by saying or doing unpleasant, cruel, or annoying things. You can refer to this action as **baiting**.

> *All through the interval, Ray was baiting poor Jack, questioning*
> *him time and again about whether he wanted to change his mind.*
> *Youths baited and taunted soldiers.*
> *Black sportsmen are the latest victims of racist baiting.*

Horse-racing and gambling

6.62 Many words and expressions used to talk about horse-racing and gambling are used metaphorically, especially to talk about politics and elections.

in the running

6.63 In a horse race, a horse that is **in the running** is taking part in that race. If you say that someone is **in the running** for something, you mean that they are one of a number of people who are likely to have it or do it, especially when you want to suggest that the people concerned are competing with each other to have or do that thing.

At 48 he is too young to be in the running for the job of prime minister.
Three of the major studios were in the running to buy him out.
To be in the running to win this wonderful holiday just answer the questions on the coupon.

out of the running

6.64 In a horse race, if a horse is **out of the running**, it is not going to take part in the race even though it had been expected to, usually because it has been injured. If someone is **out of the running** for something, they are no longer likely to have it or do it, even though they wanted to, and so someone else will have or do that thing.

The ex-communists are really out of the runnning for some years to come.
Until this week he appeared to have ruled himself out of the running because of his age.
She was divorced and had married again so she was out of the running for the money anyway.

make the running

6.65 If a horse **makes the running** in a particular race, it runs very fast so that it seems likely to win and all the other horses have to try hard to keep up with it. This expression is used metaphorically to talk about a situation in which one person or thing seems to be doing very well or trying very hard and is therefore more likely to be successful than any other person or thing.

If someone **makes the running**, especially a competitive one such as an election, they do things better or faster than the other people involved, so that the other people have to work harder to try to compete with them.

From now on it's space-based astronomy that's going to make the running.

The other two actors have been making the running.
Most of the running in this campaign has been made by the novelist Mario Vargas Llosa.

neck and neck

6.66 If two horses are **neck and neck** as they approach the end of a race, they are both ahead of all the other horses, but they are so close together that it is difficult to tell which one is going to win.

If you say that two political parties or two candidates for a position are **neck and neck**, you mean that during the preparation for the election or decision on the position, it is difficult to tell which will win because they both seem to be doing very well.

The Green Party was running neck and neck with the Communists.
Running neck and neck as candidates were Manchester and Sydney, Australia.
For months, polls showed the two main parties neck and neck.

first past the post

6.67 In a horse race, the horse that passes the finishing post first is the winner. This idea of a simple and clear way of seeing who has won something is used in the expression **first-past-the-post**. A **first-past-the-post** system of electing a government is a system in which the members of parliament are the people who gain more votes than anyone else in a particular area, and the government is the party with the largest number of members of parliament. This means that the party that forms the government may actually have a total number of votes throughout the country that is less than another party. The system is easy to operate and understand but is considered by many people to be unfair.

He demanded an end to the first-past-the-post voting system within 18 months.
...the existing first-past-the-post system.

also-ran

6.68 In a horse race, an **also-ran** is a horse that took part but that did not do very well. **Also-ran** is used metaphorically to refer to people who do not have much chance of winning something such as an election, or to businesses or organizations who do not have much chance of being successful.

It is the second largest party but it is likely to remain the also-ran forever if it goes on like this.

> *Best known for its computer printers, the company was a distant*
> *also-ran in the fastest growing bit of the industry.*

gamble

6.69 If you **gamble** an amount of money, you bet it in a game of cards or on the result of a race or competition. When people gamble, there is a chance that they will win a lot of money, but there is usually an even bigger chance that they will lose the money that they have risked. **Gamble** is used metaphorically both as a verb and a noun to talk about actions which involve great risks, but which may lead to success.

6.70 If you say that something is a **gamble**, you mean that when you start it you cannot be sure whether the result will be good or bad for you.

> *Farming is quite a gamble in these conditions.*
> *Marriage is a gamble.*
> *It was his biggest political gamble and it paid off.*

Note that the noun **gamble** is used metaphorically more frequently than the verb.

6.71 If you **gamble** that something will happen, you hope that it will happen and behave as if it will. If you are wrong, and it does not happen, the results may be very bad for you.

> *He gambled that her 21 month-old daughter would sit quietly*
> *through the hour-long ceremony.*
> *She gambled that they would never use their nuclear forces.*

favourite

6.72 When people gamble on a horse race, the **favourite** is the horse that is considered to be most likely to win. **Favourite** is used as a metaphor to talk about the person or organization that is believed to be most likely to be successful in a particular situation, especially in a competitive situation.

> *The Mayor of Ankara is the current favourite for the succession.*
> *...he was ranked as favourite for the job.*
> *The US firm had been favourite to grab the order.*

outsider

6.73 In a horse race, an **outsider** is a horse that is thought unlikely to win or even to come in second or third place. If an outsider wins, the people who have gambled money on that horse are likely to win a very large sum of money. **Outsider** is used metaphorically to refer to someone who seems very unlikely to be successful in a particular situation, especially a competitive situation.

> *There has been a surge of support for an independent candidate, Mr Alberto Fujimori, who was previously considered an <u>outsider</u>.*
>
> *Until the election campaign started, he was an unknown rank <u>outsider</u>, having left the country twenty-one years ago.*

stake

6.74 When someone places a bet on a horse race, a competition, or a card game, their **stake** is the amount of money they bet, and they will lose this money if the horse, person, or team they have bet on does not win. **Stake** and the plural form **stakes** are used metaphorically to talk about situations in which things are at risk.

6.75 If you say that something is **at stake**, you mean that it is being risked in a particular situation and may be lost or damaged if the people involved are not successful.

> *<u>At stake</u> is the loss or failure of the world trade talks.*
>
> *<u>At stake</u> are more than 20,000 jobs in Britain's aerospace industry.*

6.76 The **stakes** involved in a risky situation are the things that may be lost or gained. If you say that the **stakes** are **high**, you mean that the people involved are likely to lose or gain a great deal, depending on whether or not they are successful.

> *By arresting the organisation's two top leaders the government and the army have now raised the <u>stakes</u>.*
>
> *When science deals with the lives of patients, the <u>stakes</u> are <u>high</u>.*
>
> *Magazine publishing is a <u>high-stakes</u> game.*

6.77 Stake is also used as a verb to talk about risking something. If you **stake** something such as a large amount of money or your reputation **on** the success of something, you risk losing your money or damaging your reputation if that thing is not successful.

> *He <u>has staked</u> his political future <u>on</u> an election victory.*
>
> *He <u>has staked</u> his reputation <u>on</u> the outcome.*

stakes

6.78 Horse races are sometimes called **stakes**. This is an old-fashioned use, but it still occurs in the names of some races. **Stakes** is used metaphorically to refer to a competitive situation.

You can refer to a situation which you regard as a competition or as a risk, in which it is possible to win or lose, as a particular kind of **stakes**.

> *He was a big winner in the personality stakes.*
> *The celebrated Amstel Hotel, in Amsterdam, now has a rival in the luxury hotel stakes.*
> *I didn't do so badly in the marriage stakes.*

odds

6.79 In a horse race or a similar competition where people gamble on the results, the **odds** on a particular horse, person, or team winning is the probability of them winning. For example, if you bet one pound on a horse whose odds are 'ten to one', it is thought that that horse has a one in ten chance of winning and if that horse wins the race you will win ten pounds. **Odds** is used metaphorically in a number of expressions to talk about how likely it is that a person or project will be successful.

6.80 If you say that **the odds are** that something will happen, you mean that it is likely that it will happen. If you say that **the odds are that** someone will fail, you mean that it is likely that they will fail.

> *The odds are that your heating system is costing you more than it should.*
> *The odds are that the insurance company would not have requested an investigation.*
> *The odds are that you are going to fail.*

6.81 If the **odds** are in your **favour**, you have a good chance of succeeding in what you are trying to do. If the **odds** are **against** you, you have little chance of succeeding.

> *Buying a horse is always a risk, but are there ways of making sure the odds are in your favour?*
> *She bravely continued but the odds were against her.*

6.82 If you do something **against all odds**, you manage to do something even though it was very difficult and there were many things which could have prevented you from doing it.

> *He was young and inexperienced at the time; he took positive steps to educate himself in the jail against all odds.*
> *All his men had been killed; he alone had survived, against all odds.*

6.83 If you face huge or impossible **odds**, you have a very difficult task to do, and it seems almost impossible that you will be successful, because there are many things which make it difficult for you.

People like Jenny and Sarah will have to struggle on against almost overwhelming <u>odds</u>.
...the work of those admirable women who have laboured against enormous <u>odds</u>.
Nobody realized he was facing impossible <u>odds</u>.

Here are some examples of words commonly used before **odds** in this way:

considerable	hopeless	unbelievable
enormous	impossible	
heavy	overwhelming	

7 Cooking and Food

7.1 Many words for ways of preparing food and for flavours are used metaphorically. This chapter begins by looking at words associated with preparing food, then at words for kitchen equipment. Next, words for different ways of cooking food such as **grill** and **boil** are looked at, and finally, words for flavours and tastes.

Preparing food

7.2 This section covers words associated with preparing food before it is cooked.

recipe

7.3 A **recipe** is a list of ingredients and a set of instructions that tell you how to cook a particular thing. **Recipe** is used metaphorically to talk about a particular situation or set of circumstances that is expected to have a particular result.

7.4 If you say that one thing is the **recipe for** another thing, you mean that if you do or have the first thing, you will probably do or have the second thing as a result. This can be used about both positive and negative things.

> *When asked for his recipe for happiness, he gave a very short but sensible answer: work and love.*
> *It's a stressful job, and if you don't look after yourself, it's a sure recipe for disaster.*
> *The recipe for success in such marriages seems to be that the man should have a career which has absolutely nothing to do with his wife's money.*

The plural form **recipes** can be used with this meaning, but this is much less common.

> *Clubs are relying more and more on fitness and strength as recipes for success, at the expense of skill.*

ingredient

7.5 **Ingredients** are all the different foods that you use when you are cooking a particular dish. **Ingredient** is used as a metaphor to talk about things that cause a particular situation or result.

7.6 If you say that something is an **ingredient of** or an **ingredient for** a particular situation or result, you mean that that thing helps to cause the situation or result. This is more common when talking about positive situations or results, but can also be used about negative ones.

A good image is one of the most vital ingredients of business success.
Fun is an essential ingredient of physical and emotional health.
One of the key ingredients of a safe investment is preservation of capital.

7.7 You can say that one thing is an **ingredient in** another when the first thing is one of the things which contributes to the second thing.

He also knows that the most important ingredient in any team is confidence.

7.8 If you say that one thing has **the ingredients** to do or be another thing, you mean that the first thing has all the qualities that are necessary in order to do or be the second thing.

The novel certainly has all the ingredients to be a big success.
The meeting had all the ingredients of high political drama.

7.9 Here are some examples of adjectives commonly used before **ingredient** and **ingredients** in the ways explained above:

basic	important	necessary
classic	key	right
crucial	main	usual
essential	major	vital

slice

7.10 A **slice** of bread, meat, cake, or other food is a thin piece of it that has been cut from a larger piece. A **slice of** is used metaphorically to refer to an amount or share of something.

Note that the plural form **slices** is not usually used metaphorically.

7.11 You can refer to a part or share of something such as money or profit as a **slice of** money or profit.

Universities depend less on government grants today; a significant slice of their income is from the private sector.
Ministers and their departments will have to battle for a slice of the funds.
Giving the workforce a slice of the profit, be it in cash or shares, is a good thing.

7.12 You can refer to a period of time as a **slice of** time.

We each need privacy; a slice of time apart and alone.
A large slice of her day goes on picking up toys, feeding the baby, clearing up after her and nappy-changing.

7.13 You can use a **slice of** luck or a **slice of** fortune to refer to an unexpected event which is lucky for someone.

Even at their best, the team might need a slice of luck.
John had a slice of luck in insurance payouts.
What David needs is a slice of good fortune.

7.14 A **slice of life** is something such as an event, film, or picture, which helps people to understand everyday life as other people experience it.

Independent travel, when it lives up to its promise, gives you a slice of life as others live it.
Casual photographs taken in relaxed circumstances give a richer and more intimate slice of life than a formal picture.

7.15 If you say that someone wants a **slice of the action**, you mean that they want to join in with an activity that is successful.

The US banks are now likely to want a slice of the action.
Everyone it seems wants to know what is going on down there and how they can get a slice of the action.
Mountain bike racing enjoys a larger slice of the action than in previous years.

water down

7.16 To **water down** a liquid means to add water to it so that it is weaker or so that the flavour of it is not as strong. **Water down** is used metaphorically to talk about weakening the effect or impact of something.

If you say that something such as a plan, statement, or proposal **is watered down**, you mean that it is less forceful or controversial than it originally was. This is used showing disapproval.

...the watered-down version of an earlier suggestion.
Proposed European Community legislation affecting bird-keepers has been watered down.

dilute

7.17 To **dilute** a liquid means to add water or another liquid to it so that it is weaker or so that the flavour of it is not as strong. **Dilute** is more formal than **water down**, but it is used metaphorically in a similar way.

If someone or something **dilutes** a belief, value, or quality, they make it weaker and less effective. This is used showing disapproval.

The addition of a mechanically cheery score behind the action is another conventional touch diluting the movie's freshness.
Does any of this dilute the ideal of impartiality?

Kitchen equipment

7.18 A number of words used to refer to items of equipment used to prepare and cook food are also used metaphorically.

back burner, front burner

7.19 On a cooker, the parts on top that heat up and are used to cook things in pans are sometimes referred to as **burners**, especially if it is a gas cooker. The burners at the back of the cooker are usually used to cook things which do not need to be stirred very often, or which take a long time to cook. The burners at the front of the cooker are usually used to cook things which need to be stirred frequently or which you want to cook quickly.

Back burner and **front burner** are used metaphorically to talk about how much attention or importance a plan or project is going to be given.

7.20 If you say that you are putting a plan or project on **the back burner**, you mean that you are going to concentrate on something else instead. You have not given up the project for ever, but are leaving it so that you can take it up again later when you have more time.

> *For ten years she has looked after three children, with her career very much on the back burner.*
> *Obviously this means you're going to have to put one project on the back burner.*
> *Bearing in mind his wife's reaction to the project, he had, probably wisely, consigned the idea to the back burner for the time being.*

7.21 If you say that you are putting a plan or project on **the front burner**, you mean that you are going to give it a lot of attention and try to carry it out as soon as possible.

> *By putting tourism on the front burner, the government has opened up the opportunity for substantial growth in visitors.*
> *This approach helps to put an important issue back on the front burner.*

Note that **back burner** is used metaphorically more frequently than **front burner**.

pressure cooker

7.22 A **pressure cooker** is a special kind of pan which is used to cook food very quickly by creating very high pressure inside it. **Pressure cooker** is sometimes used metaphorically to refer to stressful situations.

If you describe a situation as a **pressure cooker**, you mean that people are under a lot of stress, which means that their feelings may become very strong, and they are likely to become angry or unhappy easily.

> *He had recently escaped the emotional pressure cooker of the communal flat.*
> *The lid on the pressure cooker of nationalist emotions has now been removed.*
> *...in the pressure cooker atmosphere of the FA Cup Final.*

Methods of cooking

7.23 Many of the verbs used to describe ways of cooking food are also used metaphorically. **Heat** is associated with stressful situations and intense emotions such as anger, and many of the words for methods of cooking food which involve heat, such as **boil** and **simmer**, are also used metaphorically to talk about stressful situations and intense emotions.

See also **Chapter 10: Heat, Cold, and Fire**.

cook

7.24 To **cook** food means to prepare it using heat so that it looks, tastes, or appears different from how it was before it was cooked. **Cook** is not used metaphorically, but the phrasal verb **cook up** is used to talk about dishonest behaviour which involves trying to present information or a situation in a way which is intended to make it seem different from how it really is.

7.25 If someone **cooks up** a complicated story, they invent it and then try to convince other people that it is true.

> *He had cooked up some fantastic story.*
> *His lawyer claims that the charges were cooked up.*
> *...clumsily cooked-up propaganda.*

7.26 If people **cook up** an idea or a scheme, they invent it. This expression is used to show that you think that the idea or scheme is dishonest or strange in some way.

> *...agreements that governments have cooked up to protect their airlines.*
> *What happens now will depend on a strategy cooked up by parliament.*

stew

7.27 To **stew** food such as meat or fruit means to cook it slowly in liquid. **Stew** is used metaphorically to talk about people becoming increasingly worried about something over a period of time.

7.28 If you **let** someone **stew** or **leave** them to **stew**, you deliberately leave them to worry about something for a while, rather than helping them or telling them something that would make them feel better, especially when you think that the thing they are worrying about is their own fault. You can also say that someone **stews in** their **own juice** when they are worrying or feeling angry about something that is their own fault and you are not going to do anything to help them or to make them feel better.

> *Should I call him? No. Let him stew.*
> *'I'd rather let him stew,' Thorne said. 'We'll get more out of him that way in the end.'*
> *That was weak of me, for I should have let Marcus stew in his own juice.*
> *I thought I'd leave him to stew in his own juice until Tuesday afternoon.*

7.29 A **stew** is a meal which you make by cooking vegetables and meat in liquid for a long time. **Stew** is used as a metaphor to talk about disorganized or unsuccessful situations.

7.30 If you think that a plan or situation is not successful because it has been made by putting together several things without considering them carefully, you can refer to it as a **stew**.

> *The budget is a dreadful stew of federal subsidies and tax breaks.*
> *...taking all they can remember of early 90's culture and throwing it all together into one undignified stew.*

7.31 If someone is **in a stew**, they are very worried or upset about something.

> *He's been in a stew since this morning and now you arrive late for this discussion he considers so important!*

boil

7.32 When a liquid **boils**, or when you **boil** it, it becomes so hot that bubbles appear in it and vapour appears above it. To **boil** food means to cook it in boiling water. **Boil** is used metaphorically to talk about very strong negative emotions.

7.33 If you say that you **are boiling with rage** or with another strong negative emotion, you mean that you are so angry or feel so strongly that you find it difficult to control your behaviour.

Gil smiled tolerantly and Cross found himself boiling with rage.
I used to be nice on the outside but inside I would be boiling with
rage.
He boiled with frustration.

7.34 If you say that your **blood boils**, you mean that you are extremely angry.

His blood boiled and his anger was so intense that he felt like
knocking down everything around him.
My blood boiled at the sight but I dared not speak.

7.35 If a liquid you are cooking **boils over**, it bubbles up so much, because it is so hot, that some of the liquid comes over the top of the container it is in. **Boil over** is used as a metaphor to talk about people losing control of their emotions.

If you say that someone's feelings **boil over**, you mean that their feelings become so strong that they can no longer control them and they begin to behave in an extreme or unpredictable way.

Adolescent emotions boiled over in a way that older people would
have been able to cope with.
By the summer of 1980 public indignation had boiled over.
He is in danger of boiling over at the injustice of it all.

7.36 If you **boil down** a liquid, you boil it for a long time so that a large part of it turns to vapour and therefore there is less of it left, and the liquid that is left will be slightly different from the liquid you started with; for example, it will be thicker or it will have a stronger flavour. This idea of getting rid of part of something, especially part which is not essential, is used in the phrasal verb **boil down to**.

If you say that a problem or a complicated situation **boils down to** a particular thing, you mean that that is the most important or basic aspect of it.

It was a 28 page analysis of the movie business which basically
boiled down to two ideas: don't spend too much money, and don't
make movies without a script.
What it boiled down to was that I understood what he was talking
about and was making the right replies.

boiling point

7.37 **Boiling point** is the temperature at which a particular liquid begins to boil. For example, the boiling point of water is 100 degrees centigrade. **Boiling point** is used metaphorically in a similar way to **boil** and **boil over** to talk about strong emotions.

If you say that someone's feelings have reached **boiling point**, you mean that their feelings have become so strong that they are about to take some dramatic action. If a bad situation has reached **boiling**

point, it has become so bad that something disastrous is likely to happen.

> *His temper was already close to boiling point.*
> *With tempers and emotions almost at boiling point, it's important to take one step at a time.*
> *It has brought the present crisis to boiling point.*
> *The situation is rapidly reaching boiling point and the army has been put on stand-by.*

simmer

7.38 When you **simmer** food or when it **simmers**, you cook it by keeping it at boiling point or just below boiling point. **Simmer** is used metaphorically in a way that is related to the metaphorical use of **boil**, to talk about rows, arguments, and strong negative emotions.

7.39 If you say that disagreements or unpleasant feelings **simmer**, you mean that they continue to exist over a period of time, often growing more intense, so that they sometimes result in a serious row or an unpleasant situation. When **simmer** is used in this way, it is often used with other cooking metaphors such as **boil over**.

> *...the row that simmered during the summer.*
> *The dispute, which has been simmering for years, came to the boil in April.*
> *Passions which have simmered throughout the year can bubble over.*
> *The authorities have managed to keep the lid on any simmering discontent.*

7.40 If you say that someone **is simmering down**, you mean that they have been very angry or upset, but now they are becoming calmer.

> *'It's the shock,' she said, 'They'll simmer down.'*
> *Ginny's initial rage had simmered down.*

roast

7.41 To **roast** meat or other food means to cook it using dry heat in an oven or over a fire. **Roast** is used metaphorically to talk about one person shouting at or criticizing another person.

If you say that one person **roasts** another, or **gives** them **a roasting**, you mean that the first person shouts at or severely criticizes the second person. This is usually because the first person is in authority over the second person, and the second person has done something wrong.

If it had been Mattie's class at the training centre, Mattie would
have roasted him in front of all the others.
There was no way Bobby should have done what he did. I have
given him the biggest roasting of his life.
He told us how a roasting from his old boss helped rescue his
career.

grill

7.42 To **grill** meat, fish, or other food means to cook it using strong
direct heat directly above or below it. **Grill** is used metaphorically to
talk about one person questioning another person in a persistent or
threatening way.

If someone **grills** you, or gives you a **grilling**, they ask you a lot of
detailed questions in a way which you find unpleasant or frightening.

The police grilled him for hours.
She kept grilling me about what my connection was with the
department.
He now faces a tough grilling and a report will be sent to the
Crown Prosecution Service which will decide whether to press
charges.

bake

7.43 When a cake or bread **bakes**, or when you **bake** it, it cooks in an
oven without any extra liquid or fat. The verb **bake** is not normally
used metaphorically, but the expression **half-baked** is used to talk
about things such as plans or ideas that seem incomplete or that have
not been thought about properly, especially if they seem childish or
unrealistic.

The vast majority of ordinary people do not want or need these
half-baked ideas about the world.
...second-hand half-baked sociological theories.
This is another half-baked scheme that isn't going to work.

Flavour and taste

7.44 A number of words used to describe and refer to the flavours and
tastes of food are also used metaphorically to talk about the qualities
that something has.

flavour

7.45 The **flavour** of food or drink is the way that it tastes, for
example, whether it is salty or sweet. **Flavour** is used metaphorically

to talk about the particular qualities that something has that seem special to it, or that remind you of something else.

>*...the cosmopolitan flavour of Hong Kong.*
>*Claude studied and worked in Rome and his landscapes have a distinctly Italian flavour.*

7.46 A **flavour of** something is something that you experience which is just enough to give you a good idea of what that thing is like.

>*Even more enjoyable is a day trip, giving you a flavour of France in just a few hours.*
>*The best way I can give you the flavour of its argument is to read you its opening paragraphs.*

7.47 If you refer to a person or thing as **flavour of the month**, you mean that they are very popular at the moment, but you are suggesting that this will not continue for long.

>*He is certainly flavour of the month as far as the French are concerned.*
>*At the moment the flavour of the month is the fixed-rate loan.*

spice

7.48 **Spice** is a part of a plant which has a strong or unusual taste and which can be added to food or drink to give it a particular flavour. **Spice** is used metaphorically to refer to a quality or a situation which makes something else more interesting or exciting, for example, by introducing a risk.

Note that **spice** can only be used in this way as an uncount noun.

>*His absences from home may have added spice to their marriage.*
>*If you want to add a little more spice to your investments then it is worth looking outside the UK.*
>*When journalists want a little spice, they call me. I've been outspoken in my life.*

7.49 If you **spice** something or **spice** it **up**, you make it more interesting or exciting by adding something to it or changing it in some way.

>*It is a moving account of his early childhood, his work in the theatre and Hollywood, spiced with encounters with stars.*
>*Those safe insurance policies are spiced up with the prospect of an extra pay-out.*

spicy

7.50 If someone describes something as **spicy**, they mean that they find it more interesting than other, similar, things, for example because it is a little dangerous, or because it has associations with sex.

I think the naughty side, the spicy side of my personality is explored on stage.
This series promises to be spicier than the previous homely tales.

See also **peppery: 7.56**.

bland

7.51 Food or drink that tastes **bland** has very little flavour. **Bland** is used metaphorically to describe people or things that seem dull or boring and have nothing special or exciting about them.

Are they really that special? Aren't they a little bland?
He was pleasant, bland, and utterly conventional.
They are hoping to add spice to a bland contest.

dry

7.52 **Dry** food does not have anything in it or on it to make it moist, for example, **dry** bread is bread without butter or jam on it; **dry** meat is not moist, usually because it has been cooked for too long. Many people find dry food unpleasant or boring. **Dry** is used metaphorically to describe information that is presented in a way that makes it seem uninteresting, especially because it does not seem to relate to ordinary people and their lives.

Many people are put off poetry by the way it's taught in schools, where it can be made to seem dry and too impersonal.
They will give brief, practical and interesting information, not just dry scientific facts.

7.53 **Dry** sherry or wine tastes slightly acidic and is not sweet. Some people like drinks that taste like this, but a lot of people find them unpleasant because they are so different to what they are used to. **Dry** is used as a metaphor to describe comments that are clever or funny, but in a subtle, unusual way that not everyone will understand or find amusing.

She'd answered with a suggestion of dry amusement.
Even when he might appear to be depressed, his dry sense of humour never deserted him.

drily

7.54 If someone speaks **drily**, they sound unfriendly and unemotional, although they may be making a joke or being ironic. This use is most common in written English, especially novels.

'Do you know anybody who doesn't cheat?' I asked drily.

Note that this can also be spelt **dryly**.

'I'm sorry, it never occurred to me.' 'Clearly,' he said, dryly.

salty

7.55 **Salty** food or drink tastes of salt. **Salty** is used metaphorically to describe language that is honest and interesting but occasionally includes swearing or offensive language.

Sam's vocabulary includes some quite salty language.
His work is dense and sharp, with salty dialogue.
She was the salty commentator on everything that happened in the ward.

peppery

7.56 **Peppery** food tastes spicy because there is a lot of pepper in it. Although the literal meanings are similar, **peppery** is not used metaphorically in a similar way to **spicy**. **Peppery** is used to describe people, especially elderly people, who are grumpy or who seem to get irritated easily.

He was a peppery old man who was a good deal kinder than he looked.
'Nothing wrong with that,' he said. He was beginning to get peppery again.
The President was in a particularly peppery mood this morning.

sweet

7.57 **Sweet** food or drink tastes of sugar rather than of salt. **Sweet** is used as a metaphor to describe people or actions that are pleasant or appealing.

7.58 Someone who is **sweet** is pleasant, good-tempered, and kind. You can describe people's actions as **sweet**.

Sweet is used more commonly to describe girls and women than boys and men.

She was a very pretty, sweet girl.
Judy had always been very sweet and patient with me.

'Would you like me to come with you?'—'That's sweet of you, but I'll be alright.'

7.59 A **sweet** voice is pleasant and smooth, and usually high-pitched.

Her voice was as soft and sweet as a young girl's.

7.60 If you want to **keep** someone **sweet**, you want to please them so that they will behave pleasantly and not cause problems for you.

Do tip the barman to keep him sweet.
The desire to keep things sweet will persuade him to go along with every suggestion that is made.

sweetly

7.61 You can say that people behave **sweetly** if they are pleasant, good-tempered, and kind.

Sweetly is used more commonly to describe girls and women than it is to describe boys and men.

She smiled at him sweetly.
'Go to sleep,' she said sweetly.

unsavoury

7.62 **Savoury** food has a salty or spicy flavour rather than a sweet one. **Savoury** is not used metaphorically, but the related word, **unsavoury**, is used to describe unpleasant people or things.

If you describe a person, place, or thing as **unsavoury**, you mean that you find them unpleasant or morally unacceptable.

...another millionaire who has acquired his fortune in a rather unsavoury manner.
...the problems which have brought him such unsavoury publicity.
Matthew is suddenly very alone without his brother and drifts around town with a group of faintly unsavoury characters.

Note that **unsavoury** is only ever used with this meaning, and cannot be used to describe food or drinks.

bitter

7.63 A **bitter** taste is sharp rather than sweet, and often unpleasant. **Bitter** is used metaphorically to describe unpleasant or negative feelings or situations.

7.64 If someone is **bitter** about a disappointment or a bad experience, they feel unhappy and angry about it, and continue to feel like this for a long time afterwards.

It left me feeling very bitter against the police.
I was disappointed but not bitter about it.
He is still bitter about the way he has been treated.

7.65 You can describe an experience which is extremely disappointing as a **bitter blow** or a **bitter disappointment**.

It is a bitter blow to have to cancel an event at the last minute after all the preparation.

7.66 A **bitter** argument or fight is one in which the people involved feel extremely angry and unhappy with each other.

Jill wanted to keep separate bank accounts, which was the cause of many a bitter argument between us.
He was at the centre of one of the most bitter rows between the British and Irish governments.

Here are some examples of words commonly used after **bitter** in this way:

accusation	criticism	fighting
argument	debate	memory
attack	dispute	opponent
clash	division	recrimination
comment	enemy	rivalry
complaint	experience	row
controversy	fight	struggle

7.67 You can say that a bad experience **leaves a bitter taste** in your **mouth**, if you continue to feel angry or annoyed after it, and if it causes you to have a bad opinion of the people involved.

This affair is going to leave a bitter taste for many governments.

bitterly

7.68 If you complain **bitterly**, you do it in a way that shows you are extremely angry or disappointed. If you are **bitterly** disappointed or unhappy, you are extremely disappointed or unhappy.

In a letter to my wife I complained bitterly that it didn't seem to matter to her.
Steve got dressed, walked out of the room and never saw her again. Now of course, he bitterly regrets what he did.
I felt bitterly disappointed.

bitter-sweet

7.69 Food that has a **bitter-sweet** taste seems to taste bitter and sweet at the same time. **Bitter-sweet** is used metaphorically to describe events or situations that have both happy and sad qualities.

There is something for everyone in this <u>bitter-sweet</u> tale.
But he's got <u>bitter-sweet</u> memories of his first appearance there.

sour

7.70 Food that is **sour** has a sharp taste like the taste of a lemon or an unripe apple. Many people find this taste unpleasant. **Sour** is used metaphorically in a similar way to **bitter** to describe unpleasant or negative feelings or emotions.

7.71 If someone is **sour**, they are bad-tempered and unhappy, often because they have had some unpleasant experiences. You can also use **sour** to describe people's expressions if they look angry and unhappy.

He was a <u>sour</u> and cruel man.
McGinnis considered this, his expression <u>sour</u>.
The door was opened by an elderly <u>sour-faced</u> man.

7.72 If something such as a friendship **turns sour** or **goes sour**, it becomes much less happy and enjoyable than it was, and the people involved start to have unpleasant feelings towards each other.

Their marriage <u>turned sour</u> and now they want to divorce.
For him, the relationship <u>was going sour</u>.

7.73 If financial arrangements **turn sour** or **go sour**, they stop being successful, and the people involved usually lose money.

They are still worried that big loans <u>could turn sour</u>.
This leaves pensioners with nothing <u>if investments go sour</u>.
They not only don't make profits, but they lose a lot of money when loans <u>go sour</u>.

7.74 You can say that a bad experience **sours** someone if it makes them unhappy and angry afterwards, so that they are unpleasant to other people.

Ralph was a terrific person; an artist who never made it but didn't let that <u>sour</u> him.
Everyone has differences of opinions but these are short-lived so try not to let them <u>sour</u> your day.
General suspicion continues to <u>sour</u> the atmosphere.

sourly

7.75 If someone does something in a way that shows that they are feeling bad-tempered or unhappy, you can say that they do that thing **sourly**.

A tall thin woman, whose mouth turned down <u>sourly</u> at the corners, stood up to greet her.

sourness

7.76 Sourness is anger and unhappiness, which have usually been caused by bad experiences, and which make people behave unpleasantly towards others.

> *His face carried an habitual expression of sourness.*
> *You will find a great deal of resentment and sourness among the workers.*

acid

7.77 An **acid** fruit or drink has a sour or sharp taste, often in a way that many people find unpleasant. **Acid** is used metaphorically to describe speech or comments which are cruel, negative, or deliberately unpleasant.

If someone has an **acid** way of speaking or an **acid** voice, they say things which are cruel, unfriendly, or critical.

> *She has an acid tongue. She can raise laughs at other people's expense.*
> *She half turned away, wanting him to stop or pause, but his acid voice continued.*
> *Max's voice changed, became acid with hatred.*

acidly

7.78 You can also say that someone speaks **acidly** if they sound unfriendly or critical or if they say cruel things.

> *'If you mean Simon, as I assume you do,' said Jeanne acidly, 'he hasn't mentioned it.'*

juicy

7.79 Juicy food, especially fruit, is soft and moist and pleasant because it has a lot of juice in it. **Juicy** is used metaphorically to describe information which is interesting and exciting.

7.80 If someone describes a piece of information as **juicy**, they mean that they find it very interesting, usually because it concerns someone else's personal affairs, especially things which that other person would like to keep secret.

> *I must say I would like to find out some really juicy secret about him.*
> *Her father dragged her into the house. It caused some juicy gossip for a few days.*
> *The whole world will be watching, anxious for all the juicy details.*

7.81 You can also use **juicy** to describe something that is very profitable.

> *He has a juicy 8% holding in the group.*
> *The fees to the bankers that arrange the issues are juicy.*

8 Plants

8.1 Things which can develop and grow and which involve groups of people are often talked about using metaphors from plants. Things often referred to and described in this way are organizations, governments, political movements, and ideas. As plants are part of the natural world, this metaphor suggests that the growth and development described are natural; sometimes choosing these words can take the emphasis away from the actions of human beings. Words for parts of plants, especially trees, are used to describe various stages of development.

This chapter begins by looking at different kinds of plants, then looks at words for parts of plants. After that, words associated with flowers and fruit are discussed, then words associated with the cultivation of plants, such as **prune** and **harvest**. Next words for plant growth are looked at, and finally words associated with unhealthy plants, such as **wither**, **wilt**, and **shrivel**.

Plants

8.2 Only a few of the words for individual species of plants are used metaphorically. The word **plant** is discussed first here, then more specific words for particular kinds of plants.

plant

8.3 A **plant** is a living thing that grows in the earth and usually has a stem, leaves, and roots. To **plant** a seed, plant, or young tree means to put it in the ground so that it will grow. The verb **plant** is used metaphorically in several different ways, all of which are associated with the idea of putting something somewhere.

8.4 If you **plant** yourself in a place, you stand or sit there in a decisive way. If you **plant** something somewhere, you put it there in a decisive way.

She had stood up. She crossed the room and planted herself in front of him.
She stepped back, her hands on her hips, with her plump shapely legs planted wide apart.
The landlady grasped Mary Ann's shoulders, planting a kiss firmly on her cheek.

8.5 If someone **plants** a bomb somewhere, they put it there so that it will explode later.

A call warned police that a two hundred pound bomb <u>had been</u> <u>planted</u> in a car in the centre of the town.

8.6 If you say that evidence of a crime, such as drugs, **has been planted** in a particular person's belongings, you mean that the evidence has been put there by someone else so that that person will be wrongly accused of a crime.

A jury decided that the drugs <u>were planted</u> on the brothers by police.
He said that according to eye-witnesses, the weapons <u>were planted</u> on the dead men afterwards to portray them as terrorists.

8.7 If a person **is planted** in an organization, they are asked to become a member of that organization, or to get a job there, in order to find out its secrets and report them to other people.

Journalists informed police, who <u>planted</u> an undercover detective to trap him.
Al himself <u>planted</u> a spy on the set while the film was being made.

8.8 You can refer to someone who you think has gone to a place or joined an organization in order to find out secrets and report them to other people as a **plant**.

Harry, at times, thought she might have been a <u>plant</u>.

See also **plant seeds: 8.52–8.54**.

vegetable

8.9 **Vegetables** are plants such as carrots, potatoes, and onions, which you can cook and eat. **Vegetable** is used to refer to people who have suffered brain damage and are unable to think or move. This is because plants are alive and grow but cannot move and do not have intelligence in the way that people and animals do.
Many people find this use offensive.

I never saw her but from all accounts she was virtually a <u>vegetable</u>.
From basically a <u>vegetable</u> he was transformed and can walk with a stick, and needs a wheelchair only occasionally.

cabbage

8.10 A **cabbage** is a type of vegetable. **Cabbage** is used in a similar way to **vegetable** to refer to people who have suffered brain damage and are unable to think or move.
Many people find this use offensive.

Now he cannot speak to us and though it hurts to say this, he is little more than a <u>cabbage</u>.

mushroom

8.11 Mushrooms are a type of fungi. You can eat some types of mushroom. They have short stems and flat tops. Mushrooms grow very quickly, and **mushroom** can be used as a verb to talk about things that grow or develop very quickly.

If you say that things such as towns or companies **mushroom**, you mean that they grow and develop very quickly.

> *A sleepy capital of a few hundred thousand people <u>has mush-roomed</u> to a crowded city of 2 million.*
> *The organization quickly <u>mushroomed</u> into a mass movement.*
> *The number of managers <u>mushroomed</u> from 700 to 13,200.*
> *He was working as an interior designer for the new boutiques and restaurants that <u>were mushrooming</u> across London.*
> *He wants to concentrate on his <u>mushrooming</u> TV career.*

Note that the noun **mushroom** is not usually used metaphorically.

Parts of plants

seed

8.12 A **seed** is the small, hard part of a plant from which a new plant grows. This idea of a small thing from which a large thing grows is used metaphorically to talk about the origins of an idea, feeling, situation, or movement. For example, you can refer to actions or events that you think will cause people to begin to feel unhappy or dissatisfied as the **seeds of** discontent; you can refer to a talent that someone has and which you think can be developed successfully as the **seed of** success.

This use is most common in literary English.

> *He considered that there were, in these developments, the <u>seeds of</u> a new moral order.*
> *The <u>seeds of</u> the future lie in the present*
> *He also carries within him a <u>seed of</u> self-destruction.*

See also **plant seeds: 8.52–8.54**.

root

8.13 The **root** of a plant is the part that grows under the ground and which supports it and provides it with water and food so that it can grow. **Root** is used metaphorically to refer to the origins of a person or situation, especially when you want to suggest that this had an important effect on the way that that person or situation developed.

8.14 The **root of** an organization, idea, or situation is the thing that led to it or caused it to happen. If you say that one situation has its

roots in another situation, you mean that the second situation led to the first one.

A good therapist will try to find the root of the problem.
Dianne insists that feminism is at the root of her success.
Where do the roots of its troubles really lie?
Jealousy has its roots in unhealthy patterns of development.
Many educational problems, however, have their roots in social and political structures.

8.15 You can refer to the town or country that you come from or to your social background as your **roots**, especially when you feel that this is very important to you or has had an important effect on you. You can say that a way of behaving or thinking has its **roots in** a place when it has developed from customs in that place.

Do not be afraid of your African roots.
...the work of eight British artists with South Asian roots.
The Japanese have never forgotten that their principal religion, Buddhism, had its roots in India.

8.16 If you say that someone **puts down roots**, you mean that they begin to feel that they belong in a particular place, for example, because they have made friends there.

Servicemen and women are seldom in the same place long enough to put down roots and buy their own home.
...a means of preventing male immigrant workers from putting down roots.

8.17 When a new idea or organization becomes known or accepted, you can say that it **takes root**.

It needs more time for its values to take root.
The beginning of an idea took root in Rosemary's mind.
Similar initiatives to encourage electric and alternative-fuel vehicles are taking root in other countries.

8.18 If you say that one thing **is rooted in** another, you mean that the first thing is strongly influenced by the second, or that it has developed from it.

Note that when **root** is used as a verb in this way, it is only used in the passive form.

Her deepest feelings were still rooted in early training.
...a socialism rooted in liberal values.

This use of **rooted** often appears with **deeply** or **firmly**. **Deeply-rooted** can be used as an adjective. **Deep-rooted** is used in the same way.

The affair was <u>deeply rooted</u> in the way the company was managed.
The organization was <u>firmly rooted</u> in the old church.
The older we grow, the more <u>deeply-rooted</u> that influence becomes.
They are fighting <u>deep-rooted</u> social and cultural traditions.

grass roots

8.19 The **grass roots** of an organization such as a political party are the ordinary people in it, rather than its leaders. **Grass-roots** campaigns or **grass-roots** support are campaigns or support organized by ordinary people rather than by the leaders.

We must insist our policemen go back to <u>grass roots</u> to restore our faith in them.
It was a <u>grass-roots</u> campaign.
There is another battle which is going on at the <u>grass-roots</u> level.

green shoots

8.20 A **shoot** is a plant that is just beginning to grow, or part of a plant that is beginning to grow. The plural form **shoots** is used as a metaphor to talk about something growing or developing in the structure '**green shoots of recovery**'. If someone says that there are **green shoots of recovery** in a particular country, they mean that the economic problems of that country are being solved and there are signs that the economy will improve in the near future.

Typically the first <u>green shoots of recovery</u> herald an increase in bankruptcy.
There would, he added, be no <u>green shoots of</u> economic <u>recovery</u> until interest rates came down.

stem

8.21 The **stem** of a plant is the thin upright part on which the leaves and flowers grow. This idea of one part of something connecting it to other parts is used in the verb **stem** to talk about ideas or situations that are connected in some way. If you say that one thing **stems from** another, you mean that the first thing is a result of the second.

The controversy <u>stems from</u> an interview given by the mayor to Reuters news agency.
Part of my pleasure <u>stemmed from</u> the fact that I knew the author.
A massive new effort is needed to fight the growth of cocaine addiction and the crime that <u>stems from</u> it.

Note that the noun **stem** is not usually used metaphorically.

thorny

8.22 Thorns are the sharp points on some plants and trees, for example, on a rose bush. A **thorny** plant or tree is covered with thorns and hurts or scratches your skin if you are not careful when you touch it. **Thorny** is used as a metaphor to describe problems or situations which need to be dealt with very carefully.

A **thorny** issue or question is a very difficult one, because people have different ideas about it and there are no clear answers or solutions. This means that the people involved have to be very careful what they say or do or they could make things worse.

> *If property and finances become a thorny issue, you may find you really do need help.*
> *The thorny question of divorce was discussed.*
> *The educational questions are just as thorny.*
> *Green consumerism has done nothing to raise the much thornier issue of how to reduce overall consumption, not just make it more environment-friendly.*

Note that the noun **thorn** is not usually used metaphorically.

branch

8.23 The **branches** of a tree are the parts that grow from its trunk and have leaves, flowers, and fruit growing on them. **Branch** is used metaphorically to talk about one thing that forms a part of another, larger thing.

8.24 A **branch** of an organization is one of its offices or parts, usually working under the authority of the central office or part.

> *...a local branch of this organization.*
> *He was back in his old job in a South London branch office.*
> *...customers using Midland Bank branches for cashing cheques or paying in money.*

8.25 A **branch** of an area of study is a small, specialized area of it.

> *Laser equipment is expensive but it can be used in many branches of surgery so the costs can be shared.*
> *As in all other branches of learning, the first step after deciding what area one wants to pursue is to learn what others have thought about the matter.*

8.26 If someone **branches into** a new area, or **branches out into** a new area, they start doing something different from, but usually related to, their usual work or activities.

> *He began the club for amateurs and in the few years since he branched into the professional game he's already produced four British champions.*

Only now, 21 years since he established his distinctive women's range, is he <u>branching out into</u> men's clothing.

Flowers

8.27 Words for particular types of flowers and for parts of flowers are not usually used metaphorically in English, except by individual writers for poetic or literary effect. However, more general words such as **blossom** and **flower** are frequently used to talk about people or things developing in a positive way.

bud

8.28 A **bud** is a small, pointed lump that appears on a tree or plant and develops into a leaf or flower. The noun **bud** is not usually used metaphorically, except in the expression **nip in the bud**. If you **nip** a problem **in the bud**, you deal with it at an early stage and prevent it from developing and becoming a serious problem. This expression is usually used about things which you do not approve of.

We monitor their progress very carefully so if anything goes wrong, hopefully we <u>can nip it in the bud</u>.
It is important to recognize jealousy as soon as possible and <u>to nip it in the bud</u> before it gets out of control.
In this way, problems that can lead to depression and even illness <u>can be nipped in the bud</u>.

budding

8.29 You can use **budding** to describe things which are beginning to develop. For example, a **budding** actor is someone who has just started to work as an actor or who hopes to work as an actor shortly.

They will run a workshop for <u>budding</u> authors on how to make, write and illustrate their own books.
He is not particularly serious about his <u>budding</u> recording career.
Our <u>budding</u> romance was over.

flower

8.30 A **flower** is the part of a plant which is often brightly coloured, grows on the end of a stem, and usually only lasts for a short time. When a plant **flowers**, it develops flowers. When a plant has flowers on it, it is considered to be at its most beautiful, and **flower** is used metaphorically as a noun and a verb to talk about the best or most beautiful part or aspect of something.

8.31 The **flower of** something is the best and finest part of it. This is a rather literary use.

> *They remembered her as she'd been in the <u>flower of</u> their friendship.*
> *I feel I can still do it even though I am no longer in the full <u>flower of</u> youth.*
> *Her majesty invited the <u>flower of</u> the nobility.*

8.32 The time when something **flowers** is the time when it suddenly begins to develop in a positive way, or when it is at its best and finest. This is a rather literary use.

> *Their friendship <u>flowered</u> at a time when he was a widower and perhaps felt lonely in his personal life.*
> *...the nation that <u>had</u> briefly <u>flowered</u> after 1918.*

flowering

8.33 The **flowering** of something is a period when it is very strong, popular, or successful. This is a rather literary use.

> *This was in the seventeenth century when modern science was in its first <u>flowering</u>.*
> *As these religions became established there was a <u>flowering</u> of art of every form all over the ancient world.*

blossom

8.34 **Blossom** is the flowers that appear on a tree before the fruit. When a tree **blossoms**, it produces blossom. The verb **blossom** is used metaphorically in a similar way to **flower**. If you say that something **blossoms**, you mean that it begins to develop in a positive way, or that it suddenly starts to become more positive. This use of **blossom** can be used in several different ways. These are explained below.

Note that the noun **blossom** is not usually used metaphorically.

8.35 If a relationship, especially a romantic one, **blossoms**, it becomes closer and more caring.

> *The relationship <u>blossomed</u>. They decided to live together the following year.*
> *It was not until he joined her for a skiing holiday that their romance <u>blossomed</u>.*
> *They met when she was still at school but the friendship <u>blossomed</u> and he began taking her out for quiet dinners.*

8.36 If you say that someone **blossoms**, you mean that they develop personally or professionally in a way that you approve of.

She had studied, worked, travelled and <u>blossomed</u> into an attractive intelligent young woman.
She was a gauche adolescent who wore anything that came to hand and always managed to look tatty. But over the years she has <u>blossomed</u>.
Harrison started to <u>blossom</u> as a songwriter.

8.37 If business or a career **blossoms**, it begins to develop in a positive way.

His business <u>blossomed</u> when the railway put his establishment within reach of the big city.
As her career <u>blossomed</u>, she kept her personal and professional lives totally <u>separated</u>.
...a <u>blossoming</u>, diverse economy.

bloom

8.38 A **bloom** is the flower on a plant. When a plant **blooms**, it produces flowers. The verb is used metaphorically to talk about people who seem very happy or healthy.

If someone **blooms** or **is blooming**, they look more attractive because they look much healthier and happier than before.

She <u>bloomed</u> into an utterly beautiful creature.
Greta is very much enjoying having the baby. She <u>is blooming</u>.

Note that the noun **bloom** is not usually used metaphorically.

Fruit

fruit

8.39 **Fruit** or a **fruit** is something which grows on a tree or bush and which contains seeds or a stone covered with flesh that you can eat. People sometimes grow trees or bushes so that they can gather and eat the fruit, and they have to look after the tree or bush very carefully so that it will produce fruit. This idea of something good or useful that you obtain after a lot of time and effort is used in a number of expressions which include the word **fruit**.

8.40 **The fruit of** or **the fruits of** something, such as success or labour, are the benefits that result from it.

Now they've finished will they sit back and enjoy <u>the fruit of</u> their labours?
This was <u>the</u> single most important scientific <u>fruit of</u> the whole space programme.
American and Japanese firms are better at using <u>the fruits of</u> scientific research.

They enjoy <u>the fruits of</u> success and live well.

8.41 The **fruit of** a partnership is the benefits which result from the two partners working together.

...the first <u>fruit of</u> the union between IBM and Apple.
Bowie's recent 'Real Cool World' is the first <u>fruit of</u> a new collaboration with Rodgers.

8.42 If something that you have worked hard on **bears fruit**, you are finally able to see good results from your efforts.

Their campaign seems <u>to be bearing fruit.</u>
Sooner or later our common efforts <u>will bear fruit.</u>
Last week their labour <u>bore fruit</u> and most achieved good exam results.

fruitful

8.43 **Fruitful** fields or trees produce a lot of crops. **Fruitful** is used metaphorically in a similar way to **fruit**, to talk about something being successful or having good results.

If something such as a relationship, a search, or an approach to a task is **fruitful**, it gives useful results, especially after a lot of effort or hard work.

They were eager to continue the long and <u>fruitful</u> association.
Our search so far has not been as <u>fruitful</u> as we might have hoped.
It wasn't going to be <u>fruitful</u> to approach him.

fruitless

8.44 An action, plan, or idea that is **fruitless** does not produce any useful results.

Although **fruitless** literally means 'without fruit', it is now usually used as a metaphor and is not usually used to talk about plants or trees.

She returned home after her <u>fruitless</u> efforts to find a job.
...twenty years of <u>fruitless</u> searching.

fruition

8.45 If things such as plans or ideas **reach** or **come to fruition**, they start to produce the results that were planned, usually after a long wait or a lot of work. This is a formal expression.

Although **fruition** literally means 'bearing fruit', it is not usually used to talk about plants or trees.

> *The plans finally <u>reached fruition</u>.*
> *Unfortunately a plan to reprint the play never <u>came to fruition</u>.*
> *You have the capacity to bring your ideas to <u>fruition</u>.*

Cultivating plants

8.46 A number of words associated with farming and growing plants are used metaphorically to talk about people trying to develop things.

prepare or lay the ground

8.47 Plants grow in the **ground**, and the following expressions using the word **ground** talk about plans and ideas as if they were plants or seeds that will grow and develop.

If someone **prepares** or **lays the ground** for a new development or for a change in plans, they prepare other people in some way, so that the developments or plans will be more acceptable or easier to understand when they happen.

> *The work <u>will prepare the ground</u> for future development.*
> *These two chapters <u>prepare the ground</u> for the critical argument that follows.*
> *Now they have signed agreements that <u>lay the ground</u> for a huge growth in trade and co-operation.*
> *Their positions had not changed but they <u>had laid the ground</u> for working together and that was very encouraging.*

cultivate

8.48 To **cultivate** land or crops means to prepare the land and grow crops in it. This idea of taking care to make sure that things grow and develop well is used metaphorically to talk about deliberately trying to develop something such as a relationship or a way of behaving, especially if you think you will gain an advantage through doing this.

8.49 If you **cultivate** a relationship with a person or organization, or if you **cultivate** a person, you make efforts to make your relationship with them as strong as possible, usually because you think that they can help you in some way or give you some kind of advantage.

> *He always <u>cultivated</u> friendships with the ruling class.*
> *She revered him as a painter and <u>cultivated</u> him as a friend.*
> *...<u>cultivating</u> business relationships that can lead to major accounts.*

...technical universities which boast well-organized courses and carefully cultivated links with industry.

8.50 If someone **cultivates** a particular way of behaving or of presenting themself, they make efforts to behave or appear in that way even though they are not naturally like that, usually because they think that this will give them some kind of advantage.

Cultivate is often used in this way to show disapproval, as it suggests that the person's behaviour is insincere.

He may have cultivated this image to distinguish himself from his younger brother.
He has been cultivating his image as a manager of ability.
...his carefully cultivated cockney accent and extravagant clothes.

cultivated

8.51 If you describe someone as **cultivated**, you mean that they are well educated, polite, and sophisticated. Note that this use does not show disapproval.

She was as well-educated and cultivated as she was beautiful.
A wealthy and cultivated American lady is hosting a dinner at the Jockey restaurant in Madrid.

sow or plant seeds

8.52 To **sow** or **plant seeds** means to put them in the ground so that they will grow. **Sow** or **plant seeds** is used metaphorically to talk about ideas, plans, or developments, to suggest that they are things that can be deliberately started or created.

8.53 If one person **sows** or **plants** a **seed** or **seeds** in another person's mind, the first person suggests an idea, often in an indirect way, in the hope that the second person will start thinking about it, and sometimes even believe that they thought of it first.

A seed of doubt may have been planted in your minds.
He had the skill to plant the seed in Jennifer's mind that her problem was not so important.

8.54 You can also use **sow** with **seed** to describe the start of a political or social change. If you say that someone **has sown the seeds of** change, you mean that they have taken an action which may start off much bigger changes.

The emphasis must now be on sowing the seeds of such a movement.
...debate that sowed the seeds of the welfare state.

By the time of his tragic murder in 1965, Malcolm X had sown the seeds of a new consciousness amongst African-Americans.

See also **plant: 8.3–8.8** and **seed: 8.12**.

prune

8.55 To **prune** a plant means to cut off some of its branches so that it will grow better the next year. **Prune** is used as a metaphor to talk about removing part of something in order to make it grow or develop more strongly.

8.56 If someone **prunes** a company or organization, they try to cut costs, usually by employing fewer people, in order to make the company or organization more profitable. If the government **prunes** public services or spending, it tries to spend less on them in order to save money.

They selectively pruned the workforce.
Government and educational bureaucracies can and should be ruthlessly pruned.
...the expansion of the road network alongside a pruning of the railways.

8.57 You can say that someone **prunes** promises, ideas, or plans, when they change them to make them less expensive or to make them easier to carry out.

The government forced it to prune back its promises.
Mr Patten promised to prune the curriculum and the tests.

See also **shed: 8.82–8.84**.

crop

8.58 The plants or fruits that are collected each year at harvest time are referred to as a **crop**. This idea of collecting a lot of things at the same time is used metaphorically to talk about a group of things appearing or becoming stronger or better at around the same time. For example, a **crop of** new buildings is a number of new buildings that appear at around the same time, usually in the same area.
Crop must be used with **of** and a noun when it is used in this way.

A crop of talented youngsters have already made their mark.
Of the rest of the new crop of restaurants, The Square in Piccadilly has had a remarkable success.
Calling on him for help would produce its crop of personal difficulties.
He came away with a new crop of customers.

Note that the plural form **crops** is not usually used in this way.

crop up

8.59 If something such as a problem, an idea, or a name **crops up**, it happens or appears, usually when you did not expect it to.

While the construction work progressed, another difficulty cropped up.
Unexpected work cropped up on the day of the next visit.
Your name has cropped up and he'd like to talk to you about it.

reap

8.60 To **reap** crops means to cut them down and gather them. **Reap** is used metaphorically to talk about getting good results from something that you have been doing.

If you **reap** benefits or rewards from an activity that you have been working hard at, you receive a lot of good results for your efforts.

This expression can also be used about bad results coming from people's actions but this is rare.

Employers reaped enormous benefits from cheap foreign labour.
Reynolds reaped the reward for his effort by taking sixth place.
Self-employment is growing fastest in areas where professionals can reap big rewards.
Cecilia's records are not yet reaping huge profits.
...a TV film that's reaped a clutch of international awards.

See also **harvest: 8.62**.

harvest

8.61 A crop is called a **harvest** when it is gathered in. To **harvest** a crop means to gather it in. **Harvest** is used metaphorically both as a noun and a verb to talk about the results of someone's actions.

8.62 If you **reap** the **harvest** of your actions, you see the results of them. This is a literary expression.

He began to reap the harvest of his sound training.

8.63 If you say that people **harvest** useful things, you mean that they collect them and bring them together to use.

We have thousands of ideas to harvest.
The harvesting of knowledge from space will be one of the great scientific endeavours of the next century.

dig up

8.64 To **dig** something **up** means to remove it from the ground where it has been buried or planted, usually using a tool such as a spade. **Dig up** is used metaphorically to talk about discovering facts that have been lost, hidden, or kept secret.

8.65 If you **dig up** information which is not well known, you discover it and usually make it public.

> *Had he dug up any new evidence against him?*
> *I've had enough reminders of my age today without digging up the past.*
> *...digging up facts and figures from Companies House and other sources.*

8.66 If one person **digs up dirt** or **digs up the dirt** on another person, the first person discovers unpleasant facts about the second person and makes these facts known to other people.

> *He claimed he had been hired to dig up dirt on the entrepreneur's controversial deal.*

weed out

8.67 **Weeds** are wild plants that grow in places such as gardens or fields where crops are being grown and so prevent the cultivated plants from growing properly. To **weed** a garden or a field means to remove the weeds from it. This idea of removing something that is not wanted so that other things can grow or develop more successfully is used in the phrasal verb **weed out**.

If you say that someone **weeds out** people or things, usually from an organization or company, you mean that they take out those people or things because they think that they are weak or bad for the organization or company.

> *This will make it more difficult to weed out people unsuitable for the profession.*
> *The police may need to establish ways of weeding out lazy and inefficient officers.*
> *Those in the motor trade who ignore women customers deserve to be weeded out.*
> *The worst material was never shown. It was weeded out by the television companies themselves.*

hothouse

8.68 A **hothouse** is a heated building, usually made of glass, where plants and flowers can be grown more quickly than they would grow outside, or at times of year when it would be too cold for them to grow outside. **Hothouse** is used as a metaphor to talk about situations where people live or work under a lot of pressure and are expected to develop skills and be successful more quickly than usual; this can make them more imaginative and productive but it can also be very stressful.

Adam admits he is happier away from the hothouse of the architectural debate in London.
The school has always had a hothouse atmosphere.

See also **pressure cooker: 7.22**.

greenhouse

8.69 A **greenhouse** is a glass building in which you can grow plants that need to be protected from bad weather. This idea of creating an environment that is hotter than usual is used in the expressions **greenhouse effect** and **greenhouse gases**. These expressions refer to problems caused by a build-up of gases such as carbon dioxide in the air around the Earth, which is causing the temperature of the Earth to rise.

Several groups of scientists have also provided evidence that the earth is undergoing a warming due to the greenhouse effect.
...the idea that it might be possible to control the greenhouse effect.
The United States is the world's biggest emitter of greenhouse gases.

8.70 Note that although the literal meanings of **hothouse** and **greenhouse** are similar, their metaphorical meanings are very different.

Growth

8.71 A number of words that are used to talk about the growth and development of plants are used metaphorically to talk about the growth and development of plans, ideas, and organizations.

germinate

8.72 When a seed **germinates**, a shoot comes out of it and it begins to develop into a plant. This idea of one thing beginning to develop from another is used to talk about the development of ideas into things such as projects, organizations, or actions.

You say that an idea **germinates** when it is first thought of, and a number of people begin to get interested in it and discuss it so that they can develop the idea.

Another equally outstanding design was germinating at Bristol.
The plans were a long time germinating. The discussion happened in 1980 and he did not act on it until 1989.

The new phase in the relationship between father and son <u>had germinated</u> on the long drive from Toronto.

germination

8.73 **Germination** is the process of germinating. **Germination** can be used metaphorically to talk about the development of ideas, but this is less common than the verb **germinate**.

The book is an account of the <u>germination</u> and fruition of ideas as experienced through a full career.

See also **take root: 8.17**.

sprout

8.74 When plants or seeds **sprout**, they produce new shoots or leaves. **Sprout** is used as a metaphor to talk about things that appear very quickly in large numbers, especially to suggest that this is a bad thing.

Concrete hotels and tourist villages <u>are sprouting</u> along the desert shore.
More than a million satellite dishes <u>have sprouted</u> on homes across the country in the last eighteen months.
Across the land, shopping malls <u>sprout</u> like concrete mushrooms.
Friendships <u>had sprouted</u> up in training.

Note that the noun **sprout** is not used in this way.

flourish

8.75 If a plant **flourishes**, it is very healthy and grows very quickly because the conditions it is in are right for it. **Flourish** is used metaphorically to talk about things that develop well and are very successful.

If something such as a business, country, or idea **flourishes**, it becomes stronger or is successful, usually in a way that is noticeable. You can use **flourish** in this way about both positive and negative things.

Exports <u>flourished</u>, earning Taiwan huge foreign currency reserves.
His career is <u>flourishing</u> again.
As the king refused to educate the public, ignorance and prejudice <u>flourished</u>.
...a system that allows the banks to <u>flourish</u> and profit.

flourishing

8.76 Flourishing can be used before a noun to mean 'obviously successful'.

There is now a flourishing black market in software there.
...the ruins of a once flourishing civilization.

Unhealthy plants

8.77 A number of words which are used to talk about unhealthy and dying plants are used metaphorically to talk about things such as organizations or situations which are not successful.

wither

8.78 If a flower or plant **withers**, it shrinks, dries up, and dies. This idea of something becoming weaker and then failing is used to talk about things such as ideas, organizations, or relationships which are not successful.

If something **withers** or **withers away**, it slowly becomes weaker and weaker until it becomes completely ineffective or disappears.

The centre parties have achieved spectacular by-election results in the past, only to see their support wither again in general elections.
They had been innocent sweethearts at a German University but their romance withered when they came back to England.
I could see her happiness withering.
The changes are likely to cause severe disruption for all the countries as the old system withers away.

withering

8.79 If someone is **withering**, they speak or look at people in a way that is intended to make them feel silly, ashamed, or unhappy, often in a way that will make them fail at what they are doing. A **withering** attack or look is intended to make the person who it is directed at feel silly, ashamed, or unhappy, often in a way that will make them fail at what they are doing.

Smith could be withering in debate.
The record is a withering attack on the fashion industry.
He gave me a withering glance.

wilt

8.80 If a plant **wilts**, it gradually bends downwards and is weak because it is dying or because it needs water. **Wilt** is used metaphorically to talk about people suddenly becoming weak, especially in a way that is noticeable.

If someone suddenly feels weak and unhappy because something unpleasant has happened to them, or because someone else has behaved badly to them, you can say that they **wilt**.

He visibly wilted under pressure.
The look the president gave the reporter made that experienced journalist wilt before his eyes.
She heard the sadness in my voice and her smile wilted.
Tony looked at Momma, his smile wilting.

shrivel

8.81 If a plant or a leaf **shrivels**, or if something **shrivels** it, it becomes dry and wrinkled, usually because it has lost too much moisture because of the heat. **Shrivel** is used metaphorically to talk about things failing.

If you say that something such as an organization **shrivels**, you mean that it gets smaller, weaker, and less effective. If you use **shrivel** to talk about feelings that you have, such as happiness, you mean that you are becoming sadder and less hopeful.

The union, which was once the most powerful in the country, has shrivelled under his leadership.
The sympathy made something in him shrivel, shrink away.
My heart shrivels in fear.
It was the kind of rain that shrivels the hopes of holidaymakers.

shed

8.82 When a tree **sheds** its leaves, its leaves fall off in the autumn because they are dead and no longer useful. **Shed** is used metaphorically to talk about getting rid of things that are not necessary or are no longer useful.

8.83 If a company makes some of its employees redundant in order to save money, you can say that it **has shed** those people. This use is most common in journalism.

Furniture manufacturers are cutting back on costs and shedding jobs.
Last year the company shed 40,000 of its 340,000 employees.
Firms have been much speedier in shedding employees, to cut costs.

8.84 If you **shed** something which you do not want or need any longer, you get rid of it or allow it to go.

...an attempt to shed all tradition.
Motoring organisations say the government is shedding its
responsibility for building motorways.

See also **shed light: 11.11**.

9 Weather

9.1 A number of words used to talk about weather conditions are also used metaphorically, especially to talk about emotions and personalities. This chapter looks at these words, beginning with words for sunny weather, then looking at words for cold weather. Next, words associated with clouds and wet weather are discussed, and finally words for wind and storms.

For **hot**, **cold**, and other words associated with temperature, see **Chapter 10: Heat, Cold, and Fire**.

Sunny weather

sunny

9.2 When it is **sunny**, the sun is shining. Most people think that sunny weather is pleasant, and it often makes people feel happier. **Sunny** is used as a metaphor to describe people and situations that are cheerful and pleasant.

Someone who has a **sunny** personality is cheerful and friendly, and makes the people around them feel happy. If someone is in a **sunny** mood, they feel optimistic and happy. You can also say that the outlook or the future is **sunny** if you feel positive and optimistic about it.

> *Everyone says what a happy, <u>sunny</u> girl she was.*
> *...the <u>sunnier</u> side of his character.*
> *By the time he reached the outskirts of Cambridge, David was in a <u>sunny</u> mood.*
> *Disappointing employment figures, showing a 9.5% rise, spoiled the market's <u>sunny</u> mood.*
> *Producers are well aware that in terms of sales, the outlook is far from <u>sunny</u>.*

dry

9.3 See **7.52–7.53**.

Cold weather

9.4 Cold weather is generally considered to be less pleasant than warm, sunny weather, and words used to talk about cold weather are usually used metaphorically to describe unpleasant people or behaviour. For more information on the uses of **cold**, see **Chapter 10: Heat, Cold, and Fire**.

frost

9.5 When there is **frost** or **a frost**, the temperature outside falls below freezing point and there are crystals of ice on the ground and other surfaces. **Frost** looks beautiful, but can be unpleasant because it is very cold and the ground is slippery and dangerous. **Frost** is used metaphorically to refer to feelings or ways of behaving which are polite on the surface but seem to hide unfriendly feelings. This use is most common in written English, especially novels.

'Did you?' said Amanda, with more than a touch of frost in her voice.
'I assume you can explain,' Magdalena said. There was frost in her voice.

frosty

9.6 When the weather is **frosty**, there is a frost. If someone behaves in a **frosty** way, they make it clear that they do not like you or do not approve of you by being unfriendly, although they are not actually rude to you. A **frosty** person does not like or approve of many people and behaves in a polite but very distant way.

The suggestion had been received with frosty disapproval.
...a frosty reception.
Her remote father quickly married a frosty snobbish woman who did not like her new daughter.

icy

9.7 **Icy** weather is extremely cold. An **icy** road has ice on it. **Icy** is used metaphorically in a similar way to **frosty** to describe behaviour that is polite but unfriendly.

If you describe someone's behaviour as **icy**, you mean that it is polite, but the people involved obviously dislike each other very much and are angry, though they are trying not to show this.

'You cheated me, didn't you?' he said with icy calm.
Vincent met his father's icy stare evenly.
We want our children to see that we can stay apart and still be friends. It's better this way than staying married and enduring icy silences.

icily

9.8 If people speak or behave **icily**, they obviously dislike each other and are very unfriendly but not actually rude to each other.

She asked him to help her but he told her icily, 'It is your problem, you sort it out.'

Unable to communicate, they become <u>icily</u> polite to one another.

snowed under

9.9 Snow consists of many small, white pieces of frozen water that sometimes fall from the sky in cold weather. When **snow** falls, it often settles on the ground and covers everything, sometimes covering things such as roads and houses so thickly that people cannot leave their houses or go anywhere. This idea of there being so much of a particular thing that it is difficult to do the things you normally would is used metaphorically in the expression **snowed under**.

If someone **is snowed under** with work, letters, or telephone calls, they have to do so much work, or receive so many letters or telephone calls, that it is difficult for them to cope and they do not have time to do everything they have to or want to.

Arnold <u>was</u> really <u>snowed under</u> with work.
He <u>was snowed under</u> with thousands of letters when he was doing his television show.

avalanche

9.10 An **avalanche** is a large mass of snow or rocks that falls down the side of a mountain. You can refer to a large amount of something which appears at once as an **avalanche of** that thing, especially when you are not expecting it, and it is difficult to deal with.

I was unprepared for the <u>avalanche of</u> mail which came in after my programme for BBC Radio Four.
He was eventually buried under an <u>avalanche of</u> criticism.
...an <u>avalanche of</u> greetings cards from long-lost schoolfriends.

The plural form **avalanches** can be used in this way, but this is much less common.

...<u>avalanches of</u> paperwork.

Clouds and wet weather

9.11 Most people in Britain dislike rain and wet weather, and words associated with wet weather are used metaphorically to talk about unpleasant or undesirable behaviour or situations.

cloud

9.12 A **cloud** is a mass of water vapour that floats in the sky. Clouds are usually grey or white, and they often bring rain or dull, cold weather. **Cloud** is used metaphorically in several expressions to refer to an unpleasant event which spoils a situation. It is also used to talk about things which conceal a situation or make it difficult to understand. Other words associated with weather used in this way are **haze**, **fog**, and **mist**.

9.13 You can refer to something which has bad effects or which spoils a situation as a particular kind of **cloud**. When **cloud** is used in this way, it usually occurs in the structure 'a **cloud of** something'.

He couldn't risk his political future by marrying into the family while a cloud of suspicion hung over it.
They had been suffering for weeks or even months under the cloud of depression.
A cloud of grief descended on the country and the world.

9.14 If someone or something is **under** a **cloud**, people are suspicious of them because they seem to have done something wrong. This makes it difficult for them to continue as normal.

I'll probably live the rest of my life under this cloud.
His economic reform programme has come under a cloud because of a stockmarket scandal.

9.15 If something **casts a cloud over** your situation, it makes you less hopeful and optimistic.

That immediately casts a cloud over the future of the other player.
The failure to raise prices also cast a cloud over the market.

9.16 If there is a **cloud hanging over** someone, they are unhappy because something unpleasant has happened, which may be their fault, and they do not know what the effects of it will be. This makes it difficult for them to be hopeful about the future.

We do not want the tour to end with this cloud hanging over us; we have nothing to hide.

9.17 If you say that a **cloud appears** in a particular situation, you mean something happens or appears which makes a situation less pleasant, or which makes it seem as if that situation will soon end. You can also say that a **cloud appears on the horizon**.

A cloud appeared over his friendship with the king.
Things were going great for decades, the distillery was turning out thousands of barrels of whiskey. Then a dark cloud appeared on the horizon: prohibition.

9.18 Note that the plural form **clouds** is not usually used metaphorically.

9.19 If something **clouds** a situation which would normally be good, it spoils it. This use is most common in written English, especially novels.

Recent meetings have been clouded by serious public disagreements.
We wanted to believe that Ted would benefit from living there but guilt continued to cloud our thoughts.

9.20 If your face or expression **clouds** or **clouds over**, you stop looking happy. This use is most common in written English, especially novels.

Trish's face clouded with disappointment.
Grace's face suddenly clouded over and she turned away.
The tramp's eyes clouded over and he seemed to lose interest.

9.21 If you say that something **clouds** your judgement or thoughts, you mean that it stops your judgement from being as good as usual. If something **clouds** an issue, it makes it more difficult to understand the issue clearly. This often happens because strong emotions are involved.

Wasn't he allowing his personal interests and prejudices to cloud his judgement?
You don't want your personal relationship with your employees to cloud your vision.
When a problem arises in a family emotions always cloud the issue.

Here are some examples of words commonly used with **cloud** in this way:

issue	mind	thoughts
judgement	thinking	vision

wet

9.22 If the weather is **wet**, it is raining. **Wet** weather is associated with feeling miserable or being bored, and **wet** is used metaphorically to talk about people or their behaviour when they seem to be gloomy, miserable, or weak.

9.23 If you say that someone is **wet**, you mean that they are weak and do not like to argue with other people, or that they do not have enough enthusiasm or energy. You can also use **wet** to describe people's actions. This is used in informal British English.

Don't be so wet, Charles.

9.24 In Britain, journalists often use **wet** to describe right-wing politicians who support moderate policies rather than more extreme right-wing ones. **Wet** is also used as a noun to refer to these politicians.

> *To advocate dialogue and co-operation in politics is not to be <u>wet</u> and unpolitical.*
> *Other <u>wets</u> are not satisfied: Lord Prior gave a warning that there could be serious social problems.*

shower

9.25 A **shower** is a short period of rain. **Shower** is used metaphorically both as a noun and a verb to talk about large numbers or amounts of things appearing at the same time.

9.26 A **shower of** something is a large number or amount of it, often appearing unexpectedly. **Shower** is usually used in this way about positive things.

> *...a <u>shower of</u> publicity.*
> *For those who are successful there are <u>showers of</u> praise.*

9.27 If one person **showers** another person **with** something such as gifts or praise, or **showers** gifts or praise **on** them, the first person gives the other person a lot of gifts or praise, often in a way that seems extravagant.

> *He <u>showered</u> me <u>with</u> presents which were delivered to the office.*
> *They <u>will</u> also <u>be showered with</u> gifts like Mercedes cars and luxury apartments.*
> *Because of his escape, attention <u>was being showered on</u> him.*

Note that **shower** cannot be used as a verb to talk about rain.

hail

9.28 **Hail** consists of small balls of ice that fall like rain from the sky. **Hail** is hard and often falls very heavily, so that it hurts your skin if you are outside in it and makes a loud noise when it hits windows and roofs. This idea of a large number of hurtful or damaging things is used metaphorically to talk about insults and criticism, and about physical objects that fall or are thrown at someone in large numbers.

9.29 A **hail of** something such as insults or criticism is a large amount of it, from a large number of people, directed at a particular person or organization. **Hail** is used in this way about negative things.

> *Officials sneaked out through a side door to avoid a <u>hail of</u> protest.*
> *...a <u>hail of</u> abuse.*

9.30 A **hail of** bullets is a large number of bullets fired at a particular person or place at the same time.

The victim was hit by a <u>hail of</u> bullets.
The riot police were met with a <u>hail of</u> stones and petrol bombs.

Fog, mist, and haze

9.31 **Fog**, **mist**, and **haze** are all weather conditions in which the air is filled with tiny droplets of water so that it is difficult to see. Both **fog** and **mist** are associated with cold weather, and **fog** is thicker than **mist**. **Haze** is associated with warm weather, and is not as thick as **fog** or **mist**. Because it is difficult to see in these conditions, these words are used metaphorically to talk about problems in understanding, remembering, or concentrating on things.

fog

9.32 When there is **fog**, there are tiny drops of water in the air which form a thick cloud and make it difficult to see. This idea of something that stops you from seeing clearly is used metaphorically to talk about things which stop someone from understanding, remembering, or concentrating on a situation or event clearly.

If someone is in a **fog of** some kind, they are unable to think clearly because of strong emotions they are feeling, or because they have taken drugs or drunk too much alcohol.

In a <u>fog of</u> misery she reached down for her suitcase.
She left in a <u>fog of</u> depression.
There was little she could say that would make sense through the <u>fog of</u> drugs.

foggy

9.33 When it is **foggy**, there is fog, so it is difficult to see. **Foggy** is used metaphorically to talk about having problems understanding or remembering something.

If someone says that they are **foggy** or that their mind is **foggy**, they mean that they cannot remember things well or cannot think clearly.

I must admit that I'm a bit <u>foggy</u> about this bit.
In my <u>foggy</u> state I decided to leave the apartment.
For no apparent reason my mind would get <u>foggy</u>, then I'd feel a distance from those around me.

foggiest

9.34 If you say that you **haven't the foggiest** or **haven't the foggiest idea** about something, you mean that you do not understand it at all. If you **have only the foggiest idea** about something, you understand only a very small part of it.

> *I did not have the foggiest idea what he meant.*
> *I had only the foggiest sense of what was real and what were my memories.*

mist

9.35 **Mist** consists of a large number of tiny droplets of water in the air that make it difficult to see. **Mists** is used metaphorically in expressions like '**lost in the mists of time**' and '**lost in the mists of the past**' to talk about events or situations that are difficult to find out about or understand because they happened so long ago.

> *Bruce Clark returned to his native USA and vanished into the mists of time.*
> *...lost too far back in the mists of memory.*
> *...hidden by the dim mists of history.*

Note that the singular form **mist** is not used in this way.

haze

9.36 **Haze** is light mist, caused by particles of water in the air, which stops you from seeing clearly. **Haze** is used metaphorically in a similar way to **fog**, to talk about things which stop someone from understanding, remembering, or concentrating on a situation or event clearly.

If you say that things happen to someone in a **haze** or that someone is **in a haze**, you mean that they do not understand everything that is happening, because they are ill, confused, or have taken drugs or drunk too much alcohol.

> *I was quite surprised at the way the day would drift past in a sort of haze. I couldn't read the paper, I couldn't concentrate long enough for that.*
> *His mind was a haze of fear and confusion.*
> *Even through his weakness and the haze of drugs he would ask for them.*
> *I spent the first couple of days in a haze of alcohol.*

hazy

9.37 **Hazy** weather conditions are those in which it is difficult to see because of a thin, light mist of water or dust in the air. **Hazy** is used metaphorically in a similar way to **haze** to talk about things that are difficult to understand or remember, often because they are not presented clearly or because they happen very quickly.

If an idea that someone has is **hazy**, they have not thought about it enough and do not understand it or have not considered the details. If someone has a **hazy** memory of something, they cannot remember it very well, often because it happened very quickly, or because they were not paying attention when it happened.

> *They did not know what they were fighting for, apart from a hazy notion of freedom.*
> *Many people have only a hazy idea of their expenditure.*
> *She had a very hazy impression of what had happened.*

Here are some examples of words commonly used after **hazy** in this way:

awareness	impression	recollection
idea	memory	
image	notion	

Wind and storms

9.38 A number of words used to talk about windy or stormy weather are used metaphorically to talk about situations or behaviour, especially situations or behaviour that affect a lot of people or seem likely to cause things to change.

wind

9.39 A **wind** is a current of air that moves across the earth's surface and which causes objects such as trees to move. This idea of a force that cannot be stopped and controlled and which causes things to move is used metaphorically in expressions such as '**the winds of** change' and '**the winds of discontent**' to talk about situations which seem to be likely to cause things to happen or change, especially when it seems as if no one can prevent this. These expressions are used in formal or literary English.

> *Muslims have not been slow to sense the winds of change blowing through the world.*
> *...with the winds of democracy blowing over Africa.*
> *...the chill winds of the recession.*

Note that the singular form **wind** is not usually used in this way.

breeze

9.40 A **breeze** is a pleasant, refreshing wind. **Breeze** is used metaphorically in the phrasal verbs **breeze in**, **breeze into**, and **breeze through** to talk about doing things in a casual, confident way.

If someone **breezes in** or **breezes into** a place, they enter it in a very casual way, as if they have no problems or worries. If someone **breezes through** a difficult situation, they cope with it successfully, without appearing to be worried at all by it.

> *He was fifteen minutes late when he breezed in and ordered himself a gin and tonic.*
> *He played to win, breezing into town to join some card game.*
> *The first time I appeared on television I was so terrified I didn't say a word. Now I just breeze through talk shows.*

breezy

9.41 When the weather is **breezy**, there is a fairly strong but pleasant wind blowing. Most people find **breezy** weather pleasant and refreshing. **Breezy** is used as a metaphor to describe people or their behaviour when they seem pleasant, confident, and cheerful, especially when they are enthusiastic or optimistic about things in a way that makes other people feel more enthusiastic or optimistic about them.

> *Under this breezy manner lies a very hard-working perfectionist.*
> *With breezy confidence, the owners are predicting forty million visitors.*

hurricane

9.42 A **hurricane** is an extremely violent wind or storm. Hurricanes often cause floods and a lot of damage to buildings and trees. This idea of a violent, damaging event is used metaphorically to talk about very strong negative emotions or actions which seem likely to affect people badly.

A **hurricane** of an emotion such as grief or anger is a very strong sense of this emotion that seems likely to affect a lot of people in a negative way. A **hurricane of** something such as insults or criticism is a large number of serious insults or a lot of criticism that seems likely to seriously hurt and upset someone.

> *...the hurricane of grief and anger that swept the nation.*
> *...a hurricane of abuse.*
> *Many small businesses will not survive the economic hurricane.*

whirlwind

9.43 A **whirlwind** is a tall column of air which spins round very fast and moves across the land and sea. **Whirlwind** is used as a metaphor to talk about a situation in which things happen very quickly.

9.44 A **whirlwind of** an activity is a lot of that activity that happens in an intense way over a short period of time and which seems very difficult to control. A **whirlwind of** events is a number of events that happen very quickly one after another.

The article set off a whirlwind of speculation.
The next day they flew to Washington DC where they began a whirlwind of public appearances.

9.45 A **whirlwind** event happens more quickly than usual. **Whirlwind** is often used in this way to suggest that something happened too quickly.

After a whirlwind romance the couple announced their engagement in July and were married last month.
Jason spent the afternoon on a whirlwind tour of Casablanca.

9.46 Note that the plural form **whirlwinds** is not usually used metaphorically.

storm

9.47 A **storm** is very bad weather in which it rains and the wind blows strongly. **Storms** often cause a lot of damage to buildings and trees, and can be very dangerous. **Storm** is used metaphorically in several ways to talk about strong, intense emotions, or undesirable situations, especially ones which appear suddenly and seem likely to cause trouble.

9.48 You can refer to a public scandal as a **storm**. **Storm** is often used in this way with expressions which are used to talk about literal storms, such as **gather** and **break**. For example, if a **storm is gathering**, a scandal is going to become public soon; if a **storm breaks**, a scandal becomes public; if someone **weathers a storm**, they are involved in a scandal but manage to prevent it from damaging their life or their career too much.

She was at the centre of a storm over the abolition of free school milk.
The photos caused a storm when they were first published in Italy.
The ministers hadn't realised the extent of the storm that was gathering when they planned this special meeting.
They put on a show of unity for their first public appearance together since the storm broke.

He thought he had <u>weathered the storm</u> over his affair with the actress.

9.49 A **storm of** criticisms or a **storm of** complaints is a large number of criticisms or complaints, usually caused by a particular action or event.

There has been a <u>storm of</u> criticism following the publication of his comments.
The decision has provoked <u>storms of</u> protest from Second World War veterans.
The film caused a <u>storm of</u> controversy.

Here are some examples of nouns commonly used after **storm of** in this way:

bad publicity	criticism	reproaches
complaints	outrage	
controversy	protest	

9.50 If something new **takes** a country or group of people **by storm**, it becomes very popular very quickly.

It's nearly twelve months since the film <u>took</u> America <u>by storm</u>.
'Windows' <u>has taken</u> other computer markets <u>by storm</u>.
'Step training' <u>has taken</u> the fitness industry <u>by storm</u>.

9.51 If you say that something **goes down a storm**, you mean that it is received very enthusiastically by the audience which it is designed for.

All the support bands on this tour are going to <u>go down a storm</u>.
I know there are some absolutely beautiful things to photograph which would <u>go down a storm</u>.

9.52 If someone **storms**, they speak in a very aggressive way.

She stormed, 'Don't you know who I am?'
'I don't believe what you just said in that goddamned call,' Horrigan <u>stormed</u>.

9.53 If someone **storms** somewhere, they go there in a way that shows they are very angry.

He <u>stormed</u> off to the bathroom and slammed the door behind him.
She <u>stormed</u> out of the room.

9.54 Note that **storm** cannot be used as a verb to talk about the weather.

stormy

9.55 If the weather is **stormy**, there is a lot of wind and strong rain. **Stormy** is used metaphorically in a similar way to **storm** to talk about situations in which people have very strong, intense emotions which often cause problems.

A **stormy** relationship, argument, or situation is one in which people often have emotional disagreements and become angry with each other.

> *Stuart and Sarah admit their working relationship was stormy at times.*
> *...his stormy first marriage.*
> *The couple had had a series of stormy arguments and the police had been called in recently.*
> *The meeting could be a stormy affair, with the debate centering on the country's financial scandals.*

lightning

9.56 **Lightning** is very bright flashes that appear in the sky during thunderstorms. Because **lightning** happens very quickly, **lightning** can be used before a noun to describe things that happen very quickly, or which only last for a short time.

> *Driving today requires lightning reflexes.*
> *Two days ago, they launched a lightning raid into enemy territory.*

thunder

9.57 **Thunder** is the loud, rumbling noise that you hear from the sky after a flash of lightning. When it **thunders**, you can hear thunder. **Thunder** is used metaphorically both as a noun and a verb to talk about loud noises.

9.58 The **thunder of** something is the loud, deep, or rumbling noise that it makes. This is a literary use.

> *...the thunder of the sea on the rocks.*
> *...the thunder of five hundred war drums.*

9.59 If something **thunders**, it makes a very loud noise. This is a literary use.

> *The horses thundered across the valley floor.*

9.60 You can say that someone **thunders** when they speak or shout loudly and with strong emotion. This is a literary use.

> *'Nonsense,' thundered the Commissioner.*
> *To his friends he was gentle: he thundered against injustice but he wept with those who wept.*

thunderous

9.61 Something that is **thunderous** is very loud.

His speeches were greeted by thunderous applause.
Sharpe's thunderous voice startled the nearest men.

Note that **thunderous** is not usually used to talk about the weather.

tempest

9.62 A **tempest** is a very violent storm. This is an old-fashioned or literary use. In literary English, **tempest** is used metaphorically in a similar way to **storm** to talk about violent, emotional, or difficult situations that seem likely to cause a lot of trouble or problems.

I hadn't foreseen the tempest my request would cause.
...the pitiless tempest of war.

tempestuous

9.63 Someone or something that is **tempestuous** is full of strong, passionate, or violent emotions. This is a literary word.

I have a steady long-term girlfriend but it's a very tempestuous relationship.
She was more calculating than her tempestuous husband.
...a rich and occasionally tempestuous commercial history.

Note that **tempestuous** is not usually used to talk about the weather.

10 Heat, Cold, and Fire

10.1 Many words which are used to talk about temperature, such as **hot**, **heat**, **cold**, and **cool**, are also used metaphorically, especially to talk about emotions and people's personalities.

This chapter begins by looking at words associated with **heat** and **cold**, and then looks at words used to talk about **fire**, such as **burn** and **flame**. Finally, words such as **freeze** and **melt**, which are used to talk about things changing temperature, are discussed.

See **Chapter 9: Weather** for words such as **sunny** and **icy**.

Heat and cold

10.2 Words associated with high temperatures, such as **heat** and **hot**, are used to talk about strong, often negative emotions. Words associated with medium, pleasant temperatures such as **warm** and **warmth** are associated with friendly, caring behaviour, and words associated with low temperatures such as **cold** and **cool** are usually associated with unfriendly behaviour.

In this section, further explanations of individual words are only given when they are words you may not be familiar with, such as **lukewarm**.

heat

10.3 **Heat** is used to talk about very strong, often aggressive feelings, especially when they are associated with a stressful or tense situation. For example, if you say that something happened in **the heat of an argument**, you mean that it happened during a very fierce argument when people were angry or upset and not thinking properly.

> *They directed the full heat of their rhetoric against Mr Bush.*
> *'Look here,' I said, without heat, 'all I did was to walk down a street and sit down.'*
> *He took a girl into the studio and in the heat of an argument, she threw a glass of gin and tonic over the mixing desk.*
> *The trouble with arguments is that things get said in the heat of the moment that are regretted afterwards.*

10.4 If you say that something or someone **has taken the heat out of** a particular situation, you mean that they have made the situation less emotional so that people have become calmer and less aggressive.

> *In a clear bid to take the heat out of the rebellion he authorised an interest rate cut.*

*Some of the heat could be taken out of Cabinet disputes if
Ministers went on a course in basic team work.*

10.5 You can say **'the heat is on'** when people are under a lot of
pressure to do something as well as possible, for example, when
football players are taking part in an important match.

You need to perform well when the heat is on.
*We kept going just that little bit better than our rivals when the
heat was on.*

10.6 Heat can also be used to refer to attention which is critical and
unwelcome. If someone does something to **take the heat off** something which is receiving a lot of unwelcome attention, they try to do
something to get rid of this attention.

*He has been advised to take a long family holiday to take the heat
off the scandal.*
*He's hoping that this will take the heat off criticism of his
economic policy.*

10.7 If a situation **heats up**, things begin to happen more quickly and
with increased interest or excitement among the people involved.

*The President will be bombarded with criticism as the election
campaign heats up.*
*Then, in the last couple of years, the movement for democracy
began to heat up.*

heated

10.8 A **heated** discussion or argument is one in which people feel
strongly and become angry.

Behind the next door a more heated discussion was taking place.
*It was a very heated argument and they were shouting at each
other.*
*One of the councillors attacked a fellow member during a heated
debate.*

heatedly

10.9 If people speak or argue **heatedly**, they feel very strongly about
the discussion and become angry with each other.

*Some members argued heatedly that they had not supported the
emergency committee.*
...one of the most heatedly debated aspects of the theory.

hot

10.10 If you describe something as **hot**, you mean that everyone is interested in it because it is currently very important or currently considered very good. This is an informal use.

There's also home cinema, the hot topic of the moment.
...a place where young Americans debate the hot issues of the day.
As investors we're looking for the area that will be hot next year or the year after.
...currently one of Hollywood's hottest box office attractions.

10.11 In informal speech, people sometimes use **hot** to show that they think something is very good, strong, or successful.

Now he runs the hottest nightclub in Hollywood.
The song is still high in the hit parade, seeing off hot competition.

10.12 In informal speech, people sometimes use **hot** to describe property which has been stolen and which the police may be looking for.

He knew the radios were hot but he hadn't grasped the real significance of the situation.

10.13 Someone who has a **hot temper** becomes angry very easily.

As a child I had a really hot temper.
Joanne worries that his hot temper will lead to violence.
He is so hot tempered and excitable.

10.14 **Hot up** means the same as **heat up: 10.7**.

The battle for the Formula One Championship hotted up.
The debate is hotting up in Germany on the timing of elections.

hotly

10.15 If people speak about something **hotly**, they speak in a way that shows that they feel very strongly about that subject, especially if they feel angry about it.

This problem has been hotly debated.
The book has been hotly disputed by experts in the various fields that it touches on.
'How many times have I told you,' I responded hotly, 'No surprises in meetings.'

10.16 If something is **hotly contested**, there is a lot of competition for it or a lot of disagreement over it.

This year's final will be as hotly contested as ever.

The figures are being <u>hotly contested</u> by the Minister of Interior,
who has claimed that <u>only 1%</u> of the workforce joined the strike.

warm

10.17 Whereas **heat** is usually used to talk about emotions which are
strong and often negative, **warm** is used to describe emotions that are
friendly, caring, and positive.

10.18 **Warm** people, feelings, or actions are friendly and caring.

You are a <u>warm</u>, caring person.
We were full of <u>warm</u> feelings about the country and its people,
who had been friendly and helpful to us.
At Trevose Golf and Country Club, you'll always find a <u>warm</u>
welcome.
...a <u>warm</u> personality.

10.19 If you **warm to** someone, you begin to feel friendly, positive
feelings towards them.

From the first, the public <u>warmed to</u> him.
At first people were afraid of him; then they <u>warmed to</u> him.

10.20 See also **heart-warming: 1.48**, **warm-hearted: 1.55**.

warmly

10.21 If someone does something **warmly**, they do it with enthusiasm and positive feelings.

He was <u>warmly</u> congratulated by his five colleagues.
The project has been <u>warmly</u> welcomed in the West London
borough of Hounslow.
He shook my hand <u>warmly</u>.

warmth

10.22 **Warmth** is used to refer to friendly and caring feelings.

These children don't even know what it's like to feel <u>warmth</u> and
love and someone to hug them.
She radiated love, good humour, <u>warmth</u> and generosity.
...the <u>warmth</u> of his family.

lukewarm

10.23 Something, especially liquid, that is **lukewarm** is not really
very warm. Because **lukewarm** things are not really warm or cold,

lukewarm is used metaphorically to talk about behaviour that is not really very friendly or enthusiastic, but which is not openly negative or unfriendly either. **Lukewarm** is often used in this way to show that you had hoped or expected that people would be more friendly or enthusiastic.

Haig had always been lukewarm about this idea.
He muttered a lukewarm congratulation.
They showed at best a lukewarm attitude and at worst a positive hostility towards public involvement.

tepid

10.24 Water or a liquid that is **tepid** is slightly warm. **Tepid** is used metaphorically in a similar way to **lukewarm** to talk about feelings or reactions that are not very strong or positive. If you describe something such as a feeling or reaction as **tepid**, you mean that it lacks enthusiasm or liveliness.

With the film opening here this week, early British reviews have been equally tepid.
Unfortunately, when she performed the reception was tepid to say the least.
They gave only tepid support.

cool

10.25 Cool is used to describe behaviour that is very different from the behaviour described by words such as **hot** and **warm**. **Cool** feelings or behaviour are calm, not passionate or excited.

10.26 If someone's behaviour to you is **cool**, it is polite but not friendly or positive.

He's likely to receive a formal but cool reception.
Mr Hans Van Den Broek is reportedly cool about the idea.

10.27 Cool people are calm and seem to think carefully before they say or do things. **Cool** behaviour is calm and confident and seems well thought-out.

What I believe we have here is a cool and clever criminal.
The absolutely essential thing is to remain very cool and calm in these difficult moments.

10.28 If you **play it cool**, you behave in a calm way in a stressful situation. This is an informal expression, used mainly in spoken English.

I thought they played it very cool myself.

10.29 Cool can be used as a noun in informal speech, when it is used to refer to someone's temper and their unemotional attitude. If someone **loses** their **cool**, they become angry and behave in an excited way. If they **keep** their **cool**, they control their temper and behave calmly, even though they are in a difficult or frightening situation.

During a Test Match the pressure is so intense she has been known to lose her cool.
He kept his cool and sense of humour, amid the tears of other jockeys and trainers.

10.30 The verb **cool** is used metaphorically in a number of ways, all of which are associated with the idea of things losing intensity, strength, or force.

10.31 If relationships or feelings are becoming less friendly, you can say that they **are cooling**.

The formerly warm relations between the two countries have cooled.
Now that the affair has cooled, he has moved back in with his wife.
He thought she had cooled towards him.

10.32 If you have been angry, and you **cool down** or **cool**, you slowly become less angry.

Tempers have cooled down a bit and I hope we could sort things out between us.
She should leave the room when her anger gets the best of her and not come back until she's cooled down.
You should each make your own lives, and when emotions have cooled, see if there's a possibility of friendship.

10.33 If the economy **has cooled**, people are buying and selling less than previously. This use is most common in journalism.

The hope must be that the economy has cooled sufficiently to relieve inflationary pressures.

10.34 If something such as a tense situation **cools off**, it becomes less tense and the people involved become calmer. If you have been angry about something and you **cool off**, you become less angry and are able to deal with things more calmly.

I think that the Scottish problem might cool off.
You're angry, Wade, that's all. You ought to let yourself cool off for a few days.

cold

10.35 Cold behaviour is not affected by fear or strong emotions, and often seems cruel or uncaring.

> *He felt the tremor run through him, then the usual cold calm had abruptly replaced it.*
> *Mother's cold aloof manner meant capability and strength.*

10.36 Someone who is **cold** does not show emotion and seems unfriendly. You can also describe people's expressions as **cold** if they are unfriendly and do not show any feelings.

> *He was very cold and uncaring about it, as if it wasn't important.*
> *He used to say to me in a cold, calculating way, 'I'm not going to leave any bruises.'*
> *Daddy watched them with cold eyes.*

Note that the noun **cold** is not usually used in this way.

coldly

10.37 If someone does something **coldly**, they appear unfriendly and do not show any feelings.

> *She looked at him coldly.*
> *The speech was received coldly.*
> *The organization was coldly efficient.*

coldness

10.38 Coldness is used to refer to lack of emotions towards other people, or to unfriendly behaviour which is not pleasant but is not openly rude.

> *During those final months, he saw a coldness develop between his mother and Aunt Vera.*
> *His coldness angered her.*
> *The coldness has disappeared from his voice.*

chilly

10.39 Something that is **chilly** is uncomfortably cold. **Chilly** is used metaphorically in a similar way to **cool** and **cold** to describe behaviour which is polite but not friendly. A **chilly** relationship is one in which people are polite, but clearly do not like each other.

> *The business council, a powerful association of chief executives, gave him a chilly reception.*
> *...his chilly relationship with Stephens.*

Wilson had remained chilly toward him.

chill

10.40 If you **chill** something or if it **chills**, you lower its temperature so that it is quite cold but does not freeze. If something such as the wind **chills** you, it makes you feel very cold. **Chill** is used metaphorically in a different way from **chilly**, to talk about fear.

10.41 If you **are chilled** or if something **chills** you, something you hear or see makes you suddenly frightened or anxious, in a way that makes you feel cold. This use is most common in written English, especially novels.

O'Day was chilled by what he had just learned.
Lynsey, chilled by the turn of events, said she had to leave for her dinner date.
The thought chilled him.

10.42 If you feel a **chill of** some kind, you suddenly feel frightened or anxious that something very unpleasant has happened or may happen. This use is most common in written English, especially novels.

Hunter felt a chill of fear run down his back.
...the chill of the unknown.
Lewis's head jerked up and he stared at me. I felt a chill of recognition.

chilling

10.43 A **chilling** book, film, or piece of information is one which makes you feel horrified, frightened, or anxious so that you shiver or feel cold.

He described in chilling detail how he attacked her during one of their frequent rows.
...the town where Bram Stoker wrote his chilling novel, Dracula.

Words associated with fire

10.44 A number of words associated with **fire** are used metaphorically, especially to talk about strong emotions such as anger and love.

fire

10.45 **Fire** is the hot, bright flame produced by things that are burning. **Fire** is very useful for heating and cooking and for driving machines, but it is also very dangerous and can cause a lot of damage if it is not kept under control. The plural form, **fires**, is used metaphorically to talk about strong emotions which can be positive but which can also cause problems if they are allowed to get out of control.

If you talk about **the fires of** a particular thing, you are referring to the very strong emotions which that thing causes, especially when you want to suggest that this may not be a good thing as those emotions could cause problems.

Fires is often used in this way with other words and expressions associated with fire, such as **fuel** and **dampen down**.

> *Behind his soft-spoken manner, the fires of ambition burned.*
> *The President warned that this will fuel the fires of nationalism.*
> *This proved insufficient to dampen down the fires of controversy.*

Note that the singular form **fire** is not usually used in this way.

fiery

10.46 People who are **fiery** have very strong emotions, argue a lot, and become angry very easily. A **fiery** relationship is one in which people have strong feelings towards each other and argue frequently.

> *Marianne and I are both fiery people.*
> *She's a fiery political figure.*
> *He'll have to keep his fiery temper under control.*
> *The lady was ten years his senior. It was a fiery relationship.*

10.47 A **fiery** speech or piece of writing expresses strong emotions, usually in order to make the people who hear or read it react strongly.

> *About twenty thousand people heard a fiery speech from the Secretary General.*
> *...a fiery magazine article.*

flame

10.48 A **flame** is a bright hot stream of burning gas that comes from something that is burning. The plural form **flames** is used metaphorically in a similar way to **fire** to talk about strong emotions, especially emotions that could cause problems if they are not kept under control.

If you talk about **the flames of** a particular thing, you are referring to the very strong emotions which that thing causes, especially when you want to suggest that these emotions could cause problems.

Flames is often used in this way with other words and expressions associated with flames, such as **fan** and **fuel**.

> *...keeping the flames of love alive.*
> *The fact is that the very lack of evidence seems to fan the flames of suspicion.*

He accused the president of fanning the flames of violence.
...fuelling the flames of hatred.

Note that the singular form **flame** is not usually used in this way.

flicker

10.49 If a flame or a light **flickers**, it shines unsteadily, often because it is weak and is likely to go out. This idea of something being unsteady or of it not being likely to last very long is used metaphorically to talk about feelings or emotions that people only have for a short time.

10.50 If a feeling such as hope **flickers**, you feel it for a very short time. If a feeling **flickers across** someone's face, you can see it in their face for a very short time.

Though we knew our army had been defeated, hope still flickered in our hearts.
Fear flickered across Louis' features.

10.51 A **flicker of** an emotion is one that someone experiences only for a very short time, or one that you can see on their face for a very short time.

He felt a flicker of regret.
A flicker of surprise crossed the boy's face.
For a second their eyes met and she thought she saw the flicker of a smile.

flare

10.52 If a fire **flares**, the flames suddenly become larger and brighter. This idea of something suddenly becoming stronger is used metaphorically to talk about strong feelings such as anger or unpleasant situations that occur suddenly or suddenly become more intense.

10.53 If tempers **flare**, people become very angry with each other.

Tempers flared and harsh words were exchanged.

10.54 If someone **flares up**, they suddenly become angry and show their feelings strongly and aggressively.

At this I flared up. 'What difference does it make?' I demanded.
Just occasionally he did flare up; not at me of course.
He thought from the change in her face that she was going to flare up in anger.
It wasn't like Alex to flare up over something he had said about her looks.

10.55 If you say that something unpleasant such as trouble or violence **flares** or **flares up**, you mean that it suddenly starts or becomes much worse.

>*Even as the President appealed for calm, trouble flared in several American cities.*
>*Trouble flared up a year ago when David had an affair.*
>*Dozens of people were injured as fighting flared up.*
>*There's a risk of civil war flaring up.*

Here are some examples of words commonly used with **flare** and **flare up** in this way:

controversy	tension	violence
dispute	trouble	
fighting	unrest	

10.56 You can say that an injury or illness **flares up** if you have had it before, or had it in a mild form, and it suddenly comes back or becomes worse.

>*Dale stayed clear of the disease for six years until it flared up last summer.*
>*I felt good but then this injury flared up.*

10.57 If there is a **flare-up** of an unpleasant situation, it begins again when people thought it had ended, or it suddenly becomes much worse.

>*23 people have died in the new flare-up of violence in the townships.*
>*...this latest flare-up in fighting.*

Flare-up is often used in this way before the words listed at **10.55**.

10.58 You can refer to an emotional argument which starts suddenly as a **flare-up**.

>*It is very difficult for two people to live in these circumstances without tension and we do have flare-ups.*

burn

10.59 If there is a fire or a flame somewhere, you can say that a fire or flame **burns** there. **Burn** is used metaphorically in a similar way to **fire** and **flame** to talk about strong or intense emotions.

If you **are burning with** a feeling such as anger, hate, or curiosity, you have that emotion very strongly. If you **are burning** to do something, you want to do it very much.

>*Forstmann was a deeply angry man, burning with resentment.*
>*The young boy was burning with a fierce emotion.*
>*Dan burned to know what the reason could be.*

burning

10.60 A **burning** emotion is a very strong emotion that may last for a very long time.

He gave his son a look of <u>burning</u> anger.
The trial had left him with a <u>burning</u> sense of injustice.

10.61 **Burning** ambitions or desires are very deeply felt and usually last for a long time.

As a boy my <u>burning</u> ambition was to become either a priest or a family doctor.
...the <u>burning</u> desire to break free and express himself on his own terms.

10.62 A **burning** question is one to which a lot of people want to know the answer and which seems very important.

And the <u>burning</u> question will be: is he still the player he was?

burn out

10.63 If a fire **burns** itself **out**, it stops burning because there is nothing left to burn. This idea of something failing or stopping because it no longer has any fuel is used metaphorically to talk about people who can no longer carry on doing a particular task because they have worked so hard that they do not have any energy left and have become exhausted or ill.

He <u>might burn</u> himself <u>out</u> and go to an early grave.
Many exceptionally bright children <u>burn out</u> on reaching university.

burnt-out

10.64 If someone becomes **burnt out**, they have worked so hard for a long time or have been under such a lot of stress that they have become exhausted or ill and cannot carry on.

Some were simply <u>burnt out</u>, exhausted.
...a <u>burnt-out</u> business executive.

Note that this is spelt **burned out** in American English.

blaze

10.65 When a fire **blazes**, it burns brightly. **Blaze** is used metaphorically in a similar way to **burn** to talk about strong or intense feelings. If someone's eyes **are blazing** with emotion, or if an emotion **is blazing** in their eyes, their eyes look very bright because they are feeling that emotion very strongly. This use is most common in written English, especially novels.

He got to his feet and his dark eyes <u>were blazing</u> with anger.
He <u>was blazing</u> with rage.
Eva stood up and indignation <u>blazed</u> in her eyes.
His eyes <u>blazed</u> intently into mine.

10.66 If someone does something **in a blaze of** publicity or attention, they get a lot of publicity or attention when they do it.

The President launched his anti-drugs campaign <u>in a blaze of</u> publicity.
The career that began <u>in a blaze of</u> glory has ended in his forced retirement.
Vivian Richards bowed out of county cricket <u>in a blaze of</u> glory last week.

blazing

10.67 If people have a **blazing** row, they argue in a very noisy and excited way.

My husband had just had a <u>blazing</u> row with his boss.
As soon as he walked in there was a <u>blazing</u> row.

ignite

10.68 If you **ignite** something, or if it **ignites**, it begins burning or it explodes. **Ignite** is used metaphorically to talk about things that cause people to have strong or intense emotions or to begin behaving in a particular way.

If someone or something **ignites** your passions or emotions, they cause you to feel very strongly about something. If someone or something **ignites** your imagination, they make you begin to think about or imagine something.

Many commentators believe that his resignation speech <u>ignited</u> the leadership battle.
Books <u>can ignite</u> the imagination in a way that films can't.
She has failed to <u>ignite</u> what could have been a lively debate.

spark

10.69 A **spark** is a tiny bright piece of burning material that flies up from something that is burning. If a spark lands on a substance that burns easily, it can cause a fire. This idea of something which is bright and could cause a strong reaction is used metaphorically to talk about people or qualities that are lively and could cause things to happen or change.

10.70 If someone has **spark**, they seem special because they are unusually lively and intelligent, and they obviously have their own ideas and can work on their own or can encourage other people to work well with them. If there is **spark** or **a spark** in a situation, the people involved work well together and feel cheerful and optimistic about what they are doing and are likely to achieve good results.

He said they were looking for someone with a bit of spark as the new technical director.
Jimmy was so enthusiastic and motivated when he was in high school. But some spark has gone out of him at college.
The spark had gone and it was time for me to leave the club.

10.71 A **spark of** something positive such as hope is a small amount of it which makes a situation seem more pleasant or more likely to improve.

For the first time she felt a tiny spark of hope.
Her eyes were like her mother's but lacked the spark of humour and the warmth.

10.72 If one thing **sparks** or **sparks off** another, the first thing causes the second thing to happen, even though the first thing might not have seemed important enough to do this.

Nicholas travelled to India which helped spark his passion for people and paintings.
The strike was sparked by a demand for higher pay.
An interesting detail might spark off an idea.
By drawing attention to the political and social situation of their communities, they sparked off a renewed interest in Aboriginal culture.

smoulder

10.73 If something **smoulders**, it burns slowly, producing smoke but no flames. **Smoulder** is used metaphorically to talk about strong or intense emotions, or situations involving strong or intense emotions, which last for a long time.

10.74 If a feeling such as anger or hatred **smoulders** inside you, you continue to feel it but rarely show it. If a person **smoulders**, they feel angry for some time but keep their feelings hidden and do not talk about the cause of their anger.

There is a smouldering anger in the black community throughout the country.
The atmosphere smouldered with resentment.
Baxter smouldered as he drove home for lunch.

10.75 If you say that someone **smoulders**, you mean that they are sexually attractive or seem to have a sexually passionate nature, and though they may not be deliberately expressing this, it is obvious from their behaviour. **Smoulder** is usually used in this way to talk about women.

Melanie Griffith seems to smoulder with sexuality.
...Isabella Rossellini, the smouldering daughter of actress Ingrid Bergman.

10.76 If an unpleasant situation **smoulders**, it continues to exist but does not get suddenly or dramatically worse.

The government was foundering on an issue that had smouldered for years.
...the smouldering civil war.

Changes in temperature

10.77 This section looks at words such as **freeze** and **melt** which are used to talk about changes of temperature. Many of these words are used metaphorically to talk about feelings or emotions changing.

See **Chapter 7: Cooking and Food** for words such as **boil**, **simmer**, and **grill**.

freeze

10.78 If a liquid **freezes**, or if something **freezes** it, it becomes solid because of low temperatures. If something solid **freezes**, or if something **freezes** it, it becomes more stiff and brittle because of low temperatures. This idea of something becoming solid or stiff is used metaphorically to talk about people or things that cannot move or which are not allowed to move.

10.79 If you **freeze**, you feel as if you are unable to move, because you are feeling a powerful and unpleasant emotion, such as fear or horror.

Joanna froze for a moment, fighting her fear of heights.
Tanya froze in horror, the shock was the most terrible she had ever known in her life.
She was suddenly frozen with fear.

10.80 If you say that your **blood freezes**, you mean that you feel shocked and very frightened or horrified because of something you hear or see suddenly.

My blood froze at the words.

See also **blood: 1.68–1.74.**

10.81 If prices or wages **are frozen**, they cannot be raised, usually because the government is trying to control inflation. If there is a **freeze** on wages or prices, or on jobs, wages or prices cannot be raised, or more people cannot be employed, usually because of government policy.

> ...plans to raise wages and *freeze* prices.
> The court also *froze* all their assets worldwide.
> ...the 1% pay *freeze* imposed on the public sector.
> There is to be a *freeze* on government jobs.
> Alternatives could include a *freeze* on interest payments

10.82 The verb **freeze** is associated with cold and low temperatures, and **freeze** can be used metaphorically in a similar way to **cold** and **chilly**, to talk about people behaving in an unpleasant or unfriendly way.

If you **freeze** someone **out**, you ignore them so that they no longer feel part of the group of friends or colleagues that you are in, or you prevent them from taking part in something.

> I started by *freezing* her *out* and keeping information from her.
> He has sworn that he *will freeze* Cuba *out* of the world economy.

melt

10.83 If a substance **melts**, or if something **melts** it, it changes into a liquid, usually because it has been heated. **Melt** is used metaphorically to talk about negative, unfriendly feelings, which can be talked about using words such as **cold** and **cool**, changing into positive, friendly feelings, which can be talked about using words such as **warm**.

If a negative feeling which you have **melts** or **melts away**, it goes away slowly and you start to feel much more positive. If someone **melts** your **heart**, they behave in a way that makes you feel very warm and friendly towards them, even though you might not have liked them before.

> She smiled at us and I felt my disappointment *melt away*.
> Intolerance between the generations *melts away* once there are grandchildren.
> I'm sure if she read your interview her *heart would have melted* a little.
> ...a smile that *could melt my heart*.

10.84 When substances such as snow **melt**, they turn into water and disappear. **Melt** is used metaphorically in expressions such as **melt away** and **melt into** to talk about people or things that seem to disappear.

If people **melt away**, or **melt into** something such as a crowd, they go slowly so that you do not actually see them go and are not sure where they have gone. If you **melt into the background**, you mix with other people and try to behave in the same way as them, so that you will not be noticeable.

> *A group of medical staff stood next to the desk; as I moved towards them doctors and nurses seemed to melt away.*
> *The band stopped playing and melted away into the crowd.*
> *Desmond opened the door and stepped out to melt into the darkness.*
> *...places where people could melt into the background.*

thaw

10.85 When ice, snow, or something that is frozen **thaws**, it melts. If there is a **thaw**, ice and snow that are on the ground melt. **Thaw** is used metaphorically both as a noun and a verb in a similar way to **melt** to talk about negative or unfriendly feelings changing into positive or friendly ones.

10.86 If a relationship between two countries or groups of people that has been bad in the past begins to improve and become more friendly, you can say that there is a **thaw** in that relationship.

> *The decision indicates a thaw in relations between the two countries.*
> *There has been a slight thaw in such areas as scientific and cultural cooperation in the last year or two.*

10.87 If a bad relationship between two or more people or groups of people **is thawing**, it is showing signs of improving and the people involved are behaving in a more positive way towards each other. This use is most common in journalism.

> *Trade relations between America and the EC are thawing.*

10.88 If a person who has been unfriendly or unhelpful towards you **thaws**, they begin to be more friendly, helpful, and positive towards you.

> *Hillsden smiled. He felt she was beginning to thaw a little.*
> *When Peter began to show signs of talent and success, his dad began to thaw.*

11 Light, Darkness, and Colour

11.1 This chapter looks at the metaphorical uses of words which are associated with light, darkness, and colour, beginning with **light** and associated words such as **bright** and **dazzle**. Next, words such as **dark** and **gloomy** are discussed, and finally **colour** and words for particular colours such as **black** and **green**.

Light

light

11.2 The adjective **light** has two main literal uses: one is to describe objects which do not weigh very much (this is the opposite of **heavy**); the other is to describe things that are bright or well-lit (this is the opposite of **dark**).

These two literal meanings have led to two main metaphorical uses. One is to describe things that are cheerful or not serious, and the other is to describe things which are to do with intelligence or understanding. It is interesting to note that the two words which are opposite in meaning to the literal uses of **light**, **heavy** and **dark**, are also used metaphorically with the opposite meanings to the two metaphorical uses of **light**.

11.3 Objects that are **light** do not weigh very much and are therefore not very heavy. **Heavy** is used metaphorically to describe things such as books or situations that are serious or difficult. **Light** is used to describe things that are cheerful or not very serious.

11.4 If you describe your mood or personality as **light**, you mean that you feel happy and you are not worried about serious things.

> *'It was sad and emotional but there were lighter moments too,'*
> *said Jane.*
> *Develop this lighter side of your personality.*

See also **1.50–1.55**

11.5 If you try to **make light of** a serious situation, you try to make yourself happier by looking for its less serious aspects or by pretending that your problems are not very important.

> *But his mother said yesterday: 'When Michael talks like that, it*
> *means he's worried and is trying to make light of it.'*
> *Although I made light of it at the time, I knew the journey would*
> *be long and difficult.*

11.6 Sometimes in a serious or tense situation something amusing or less serious happens which makes you worry less or feel less tense. You can describe the amusing event or thing as **light relief**.

Whatever you may think about today's officials, they have been known to provide moments of light relief during games of high tension.
Those of us who have no interest in sport will not be able to rely on television for some light relief, either.

11.7 Journalists sometimes use the expression **on a lighter note** to show that they are changing the subject from serious news to news that is less serious, such as sport.

The main headline says this would halve NATO's nuclear force in Europe. On a lighter note, several of the papers have front page reports on the World Cup match in which England beat Cameroon by three goals to two.
Let's leave on a slightly lighter note.

11.8 Light is the brightness that lets you see things. **Light** comes from sources such as the sun, the moon, lamps, and fire. Because it helps you to see, and because seeing is associated with understanding and judgement, **light** is used metaphorically to talk about understanding or judging people or situations.

11.9 If you understand or think about someone or something **in a** particular kind of **light**, you think about them in that way.

It was only that now she was seeing them in a different light.
I was impressed by his dedication, I saw him in a completely new light.
Whatever really happened, people like to remember themselves in the best possible light.
'What worries me,' he said, 'is that this is going to portray John in a bad light.

Here are some examples of adjectives often used before **light** in this way:

bad	harsh	sympathetic
best	negative	unfavourable
better	new	unflattering
different	poor	worse
favourable	same	worst
good	similar	

11.10 If you say that you are thinking or acting **in the light of** a particular thing or **in light of** a particular thing, you mean that you are considering that thing when you are forming your opinions or deciding what to do.

We need to think about what we are doing in the light of our own history and today's world.
In light of the interest in the topic, it is surprising to learn how little has been written.

Such an agreement must be considered in light of the financial stability of the buyer.

11.11 If a new piece of information **sheds** or **throws light on** a particular thing, the information makes that thing easier to understand, or makes you think about it in a new way.

The report itself sheds some light on the mysterious workings of the international arms trade.
This book will, I hope, shed some light on this important if, as yet, ill-understood area of nutrition, and so help us to live more healthy lives.
There's news this week of two studies throwing new light on quakes which have, at various times, rocked parts of California.

11.12 If a piece of information **comes to light** or **is brought to light**, that information is discovered, or it is made public. If a situation **comes to light** or **is brought to light**, something happens which makes people aware of that situation.

The investigation began several weeks ago following information which came to light during an inquiry into another senior officer.
I wanted to describe it in a way that really made sense, and show something that hadn't been brought to light before.
In the last fifteen years there has been increasing evidence of athletes using drugs to boost their performance, and this problem was brought to light dramatically at the Seoul Olympics in 1988.

11.13 If something **sees the light of day** at a particular time, it comes into existence or is made known to the public at that time.

This extraordinary document first saw the light of day in 1966.
Karyn White is currently putting the finishing touches to a new album which should see the light of day later this summer.

11.14 If someone's face **lights up**, they suddenly look happy and lively.

Beryl's plain face lit up at the mention of her husband.
The old man's eyes lit up as his daughter-in-law made some laughing remark.

lighten

11.15 If something **lightens**, or if you **lighten** it, it becomes lighter or less dark in colour. As **dark** is associated with serious or unhappy situations and **light** is associated with cheerful situations, **lighten** is used metaphorically to talk about things that make situations seem less serious or unhappy.

If something **lightens** someone's mood, it makes them feel happier. If something **lightens** a tense or serious situation, it makes that situation seem less tense or serious.

> *The sun was streaming in through the window, yet it did nothing to lighten his mood.*
> *These statistics are unlikely to lighten the economic gloom.*
> *Anthony felt the need to lighten the atmosphere.*

bright

11.16 A **bright** light shines strongly. A **bright** object shines strongly or has a strong, light colour. A **bright** place is full of light. **Bright** has two main metaphorical uses, both of which are associated with metaphorical uses of **light**: one is associated with being cheerful or positive; the other is associated with intelligence.

11.17 If you describe something as **bright**, you mean that it makes you happy and confident or optimistic. If you feel **bright**, you feel cheerful and optimistic.

> *There was brighter news for the Government over Europe yesterday.*
> *...a bright cheerful voice.*
> *If I'm feeling bright and confident, I love going to parties on my own.*

11.18 If you say that the future looks **bright**, you think that things will develop well and be successful.

> *The process offered them opportunities and hopes for a brighter future.*
> *In the early days of independence, prospects for investment looked bright.*
> *People live longer nowadays, and they are better educated, and they have brighter opportunities.*
> *The 14-year-old American is hailed as one of the country's brightest hopes.*

11.19 Journalists sometimes use **on a bright note** or **on a brighter note** to show that something is positive. For example, if a journalist says that a situation ended **on a bright note**, this means that the situation ended in a way that made people feel positive or optimistic; journalists sometimes say **'on a brighter note'** to show that they are moving from bad news to good news.

> *Generally, the Stock Market ended on a bright note yesterday.*
> *On a brighter note, retail sales in the three months to October rose by an annual rate of 3.6%.*

11.20 If you look **on the bright side** of a situation, you concentrate on the positive aspects of it and try not to think about the negative ones.

I tried to look on the bright side, to be grateful that I was healthy.
Those who are committed to staying away from tobacco will never take even one cigarette, realizing that if they smoke one cigarette, they will be hooked again. But on the brighter side, the longer one stays away from the cigarettes, the easier it gets.

11.21 **Bright** can also mean intelligent. A **bright** person is clever and seems to learn or understand things quickly.

...a very bright five year old who goes to primary school.
The most popular speaker seems to be an impressively bright and energetic woman called Ms Lunn.

11.22 A **bright** idea is clever and original.

Then someone had the bright idea of adding sets of pictures, and cigarette cards spread to this country in the early 1900s.
There are lots of books crammed with bright ideas.

11.23 **Bright** is sometimes used in this way ironically, to show that you think that an idea someone has had was silly or not very practical.

This is pretty much a guaranteed waste of time. But it was the captain's bright idea.
If you get any bright ideas, tell me what they are before you do anything.

brighten

11.24 If a light **brightens**, or if a place **brightens**, it becomes lighter or brighter. **Brighten** is used metaphorically in a similar way to **bright** to talk about a situation becoming more pleasant or positive.

11.25 If something or someone **brightens** a situation, or **brightens up** a situation, they make it more pleasant.

...a laugh and a joke to brighten the day.
He's certainly brightened up an otherwise dull Saturday afternoon!

11.26 If your spirits **brighten**, or if something **brightens** them, you begin to feel more happy and optimistic.

She turned to face him. He brightened at once.
He brightened when I slipped two five-dinar notes across the countertop.
The newspapers also brought political news that brightened Franklin's spirits.

brilliant

11.27 A **brilliant** light shines very brightly. A **brilliant** colour is extremely bright. **Brilliant** is used metaphorically in a similar way to **bright**, to talk about people or things that are extremely clever or successful.

11.28 A **brilliant** person, idea, or performance is extremely clever or skilful.

> *From the start he was a brilliant student.*
> *He was considered a brilliant director.*
> *The idea was brilliant, and it later proved to be one of the greatest breakthroughs in aeronautical design since the invention of the jet engine.*
> *It was his brilliant performance in 'My Left Foot' that established his reputation.*

11.29 In informal British English, you can say something is **brilliant** when you are very pleased about it or think that it is very good.

> *The food was brilliant.*
> *His live show was brilliant.*

dazzle

11.30 If a bright light **dazzles** you, it makes you unable to see properly for a short time. **Dazzle** is used metaphorically in a similar way to **bright** and **brilliant** to talk about people or things that are extremely clever, skilful, or talented.

If something or someone **dazzles** people, those people are very impressed by the skill, talent, beauty, or other good qualities of that thing or person. Sometimes **dazzle** is used to suggest that these qualities are very impressive when people first see them, but are not really as good or as impressive as they first appear.

> *...players who dazzled crowds with their skill.*
> *She looked every inch a top model as she dazzled guests at a charity fashion show.*
> *Don't be dazzled by low interest rates.*

dazzling

11.31 If you describe someone's achievement or a sporting or theatrical performance as **dazzling**, you mean that it impresses people a great deal.

> *...these 25 years of dazzling economic success.*
> *...playing dazzling football.*

shine

11.32 When the sun or a light **shines**, it gives out a bright light. Like **bright**, **brilliant**, and **dazzle**, **shine** is used to talk about people being clever or skilful.

If someone **shines** at a skill or activity, they do it extremely well, so that other people notice them and are impressed by them.

> *Most kids have one skill at school and that means they can shine at something at least.*
> *She shines as an athlete and as an artist.*

Darkness

dark

11.33 When it is **dark**, there is not enough light to see properly, for example, because it is night. The **dark** is associated with feelings of unhappiness, depression, and despair, or with things that are unpleasant or evil. Because it is difficult to see in the dark, it is also associated with lack of knowledge and secrecy.

11.34 If you have **dark** moods or feelings, you are depressed, very unhappy, and sometimes angry.

> *He felt the same dark mood coming over him as had taken control last night.*
> *...dark despair.*

11.35 If you have **dark** thoughts, your thoughts are angry, suspicious, and unhappy.

> *He had been reluctant to go home to the bungalow, with the dark thoughts still going round in his head concerning the death of Sarah Ellis.*
> *...a place which we children regarded with dark suspicion and rarely visited.*

11.36 If you say that something has a **dark side**, or a **dark aspect**, you mean that although that thing appears good or positive, there are other, less pleasant or positive aspects of it which many people may not be aware of.

> *...the dark side of traditional married life.*
> *She, too, has a dark side.*
> *Many comedians have deeper, darker sides to their natures.*
> *...exposing the darker aspects of its past.*

11.37 A **dark** period of time is unpleasant or frightening.

> *Dark times were in store for the country and for the people.*

But back then, in the dark days following the accident, Mike could hardly begin to see how he would cope alone.
...the dark years under communism.

11.38 If you describe a period of time as your **darkest hour**, you mean that you were very unhappy at that time and that it seemed like the worst part of your life. This use is most common in written English.

John has been by her side throughout her darkest hours.
He endured his darkest hour as a trainer on the course when Private Views, the best horse he has ever trained, fell and broke its back.
...the suffering and courage of the civilian population in the country's darkest hours.

11.39 If you describe something as **dark**, you mean that it is related to things that are serious or unpleasant.

Under hypnosis you can be forced to reveal your darkest secrets.
It's a darker, more disturbing work with little in the way of light relief.
It's important not to overlook the darker realities of those enormous changes to society, like the cruel conditions endured by workers in the mines and factories.

11.40 If you are **in the dark** about something, you do not know anything about it, often because someone has deliberately avoided telling you about it.

We were kept in the dark and we didn't have staff meetings.
I'm as much in the dark as you are, I'm afraid.
At first I managed to keep my parents in the dark about missing classes.

darkly

11.41 If someone says something **darkly**, they say it in a mysterious way that suggests that they know that something unpleasant might happen.

'There are things,' he said darkly, 'that are better not said on the telephone.'
...publishers talk darkly of threats to educational standards.

darken

11.42 If something **darkens**, or if something **darkens** it, it becomes darker. **Darken** is used metaphorically in a similar way to **dark** to talk about things that are unpleasant or which make you feel unhappy.

11.43 If something bad **darkens** your life or your feelings, that bad thing makes you so unhappy that you cannot enjoy anything else.

> *This one sorrow darkens their life.*
> *But as time runs out, the prospect of war will increasingly darken the New Year.*

11.44 If your feelings **darken**, something bad makes you feel unhappy and prevents you from enjoying other things.

> *Back in his own home, the mood darkened again.*

11.45 If someone's face or expression **darkens**, they begin to look unhappy or angry.

> *He grinned at the memory, and then his face darkened.*
> *His expression changed, darkened.*

shadow

11.46 A **shadow** is a dark shape on a surface that is made when something stands between the surface and a light. If you are in **shadow**, you are in an area of darkness caused by something preventing light from reaching it. **Shadow** is used metaphorically in a way that is related to the metaphorical uses of **dark**, to talk about unpleasant or negative feelings, especially when they are caused by something particular such as an unpleasant event or a threatened action.

11.47 If people are living in **the shadow of** an unpleasant event or situation, that event or situation is making them feel unhappy or stopping them from doing the things that they really want to. If an event or situation **casts** a **shadow** over something, that event or situation is making people feel unhappy or stopping them from feeling optimistic.

> *...countries only now emerging from the shadows of the Second World War.*
> *The Archbishop, Dr Robert Runcie, said the Christmas celebration of peace this year takes place with the shadow of war looming.*
> *...the shadows cast by momentous events.*
> *The past is still casting long shadows.*

11.48 If one person lives **in** the **shadow** of another, the second person is a major influence on the first person, whose own personality is not allowed to develop fully as a result of this.

Until his premature death from tuberculosis in 1927, Gris worked entirely in the shadow of Picasso.
Sandra visibly glows in his presence—she certainly doesn't live in his shadow.

11.49 Your **shadow** is a flat dark, flat patch of shade that has a similar shape to you. Because your shadow does not have your character or personality and it only gives an impression of how you appear, **shadow** is used metaphorically to talk about people who seem less strong or capable than they used to be.

If you say that someone is a **shadow of** something that they used to be or do, or a **shadow of** their **former self**, you mean that they are now much less effective or forceful that they were in the past.

Middlesex, now a shadow of the side that dominated English county cricket in the early 1980s, were brushed aside at Southampton.
Their army is only a shadow of its former self.

11.50 You cannot avoid having a shadow in situations where it is light, and it seems as if your **shadow** goes everywhere with you; for example, when you are walking along the road it moves with you. This idea of constantly being followed is used metaphorically in the verb **shadow**.

11.51 If someone **is being shadowed**, they are being followed secretly by people such as the police.

He was being shadowed and whoever was following him didn't seem to mind if he realized it.
She was shadowed constantly by a variety of security agencies.

11.52 When journalists say that one currency **shadows** another, they mean that the value of the first currency is linked in some way to the value of the second.

The government was now committed to shadowing the Deutschmark.

11.53 In Britain, the **shadow** cabinet and **shadow** ministers are members of the main opposition party. Their job is to make statements about government policy in particular areas.

The opposition have a shadow administration waiting to take over.
...the shadow Chancellor.

gloom

11.54 **Gloom** is a state when it is nearly dark, but not completely dark. Like the related word, **dark**, **gloom** is used metaphorically to talk about feelings of unhappiness or despair.

> *There is a tremendous sense of joy here after two days of the deepest gloom.*
> *This means the country might see a fast recovery from economic gloom.*

gloomy

11.55 If a place is **gloomy**, it is almost dark so that it is difficult to see very well. **Gloomy** is used metaphorically in a similar way to **gloom**, to talk about unpleasant or negative feelings or situations.

11.56 If you describe someone's mood as **gloomy**, you mean that they are unhappy and do not seem hopeful about the future.

> *The mood is quite gloomy and I think that people are becoming really desperate.*
> *They are gloomy about their chances of success.*

11.57 If a situation is **gloomy**, it does not give you much hope of success or happiness. This metaphor is frequently used by journalists writing about economics.

> *The main story in several papers is a gloomy assessment of Britain's economy.*
> *World Health experts are painting a gloomy picture for the nineties, unless more cash can be found to combat disease.*

Colour

11.58 This section looks at the metaphorical uses of **colour**, related words such as **colourful**, and a number of words for particular colours.

Note that these words are spelt **color**, **colorful** in American English.

colour

11.59 The **colour** of something is the way that it looks because of the way it reflects light. **Blue**, **red**, and **yellow** are colours. Things that are a particular colour, or pictures that contain a lot of different colours, are often considered to be more attractive or interesting than things that are just black or white. **Colour** is used metaphorically to talk about qualities that make something more lively or interesting.

> *She had resumed the travel necessary to add depth and colour to her novels.*

Practise your speech out loud so you can hear what it sounds like and can add <u>colour</u> to it by varying your tone of voice.

11.60 To **colour** something means to change its colour, for example, by using a substance such as dye or paint. The verb **colour** is used metaphorically to talk about things that change or influence the way someone thinks about or judges things. For example, if an experience **colours** your view of a particular person, it influences and changes the way you think about that person.

Cooper's experiences in Europe <u>coloured</u> his perceptions of home.
It is religion more than anything else, which <u>colours</u> their understanding of the universe.
His recollections of their meetings <u>are coloured</u> by the tragedy.

colourful

11.61 An object that is **colourful** has bright colours or a lot of different colours. **Colourful** objects are eyecatching, although some people prefer plain objects because they think that colourful things are too bright. This idea of being noticeable in a way that some people might not approve of is used metaphorically to describe people or behaviour which is lively and interesting, often in a way that some people would disapprove of.

11.62 A **colourful** character is someone who behaves in a lively and amusing way, but who may shock some people.

Joe, who worked for a number of years with us, was a <u>colourful</u> and unique character not afraid to speak his mind.
Casey Stengal was probably the most <u>colourful</u> character in baseball.

11.63 If someone has had a **colourful** past or a **colourful** career, they have been involved in exciting but often slightly shocking things.

They have quite a <u>colourful</u> past, but I dare say that goes for most of our old families.
He could now be facing the end of a long and <u>colourful</u> career.
...a well-known City business man with a rather <u>colourful</u> background.

11.64 A **colourful** story is full of exciting details.

There are <u>colourful</u> accounts of the return to Southampton of the yacht, Maiden, with her all-woman crew.
The papers offer <u>colourful</u> descriptions of the inauguration of the President.

11.65 Colourful language is rude or offensive language; people often use **colourful** in this way to show that they are not really shocked by this language.

There was much hostility and a great deal of <u>colourful</u> language was used.

colourless

11.66 Something that is **colourless** has no colour at all. **Colourless** is used metaphorically in the opposite way to **colourful**, to say that someone or something is not very interesting or exciting. This use shows disapproval.

Some people find him lacking in personality, <u>colourless</u> perhaps.
His political opinions were as <u>colourless</u> as his personality.
...some of the most <u>colourless</u> and drab places she had ever found herself in.

black

11.67 Something that is **black** is of the darkest colour that there is, like the colour of the sky at night when there is no light at all. **Black** is associated with darkness, and many of its metaphorical uses are similar to those of **dark**. For example, it is used to talk about unhappy feelings or situations and unpleasant thoughts or situations.

11.68 If someone is in a **black** mood, they feel very miserable and depressed.

His mood grew <u>blacker</u>.
She alone could cheer him up when he was in the <u>blackest</u> depression.
...the <u>black</u> despair that finally drove her to suicide.

11.69 If you describe a period of time as **black**, you mean that it is a very unhappy or unsuccessful period, possibly the worst you have ever experienced.

He stuck with the club during the <u>black</u> periods.
Last Wednesday was one of the <u>blackest</u> days of my political career.
...the <u>blackest</u> month of the war.
The future for the industry looks even <u>blacker</u>.

11.70 Black humour involves laughing at frightening or unpleasant things such as death or war.

...<u>black</u> humour that lightens the carnage.

...a shocking black comedy, perhaps the most controversial movie in 1992.

11.71 Black thoughts or acts are very cruel or wicked. This is a literary use.

I think their crime is a blacker one than mere exploitation.

blacken

11.72 To **blacken** something means to make it black or very dark in colour. The colour black is associated with negative things, and **blacken** is used metaphorically to talk about things that destroy or damage a person's reputation or character. For example, if someone tries to **blacken** your character, they tell other people bad stories about you so that you will get a bad reputation.

...an effort to blacken my character.
Why have they gone to such lengths to blacken her name?

Here are some examples of nouns that are commonly used after **blacken** in this way:

character	name	reputation
image		

white

11.73 Something that is **white** is the palest colour that there is, like the colour of snow or milk. Whilst **black** is associated with negative things such as unhappiness, depression, and unpleasant or evil acts, **white** is associated with positive, honest behaviour.

If you describe someone's character as **whiter than white**, you mean that you have not heard any bad reports about their behaviour and they have a reputation for always behaving honestly and morally.

There was no point in inventing a whiter than white character.
She emerges from this biography whiter than white.

black and white

11.74 Black is a very dark colour, and **white** is a very pale colour, and it is very easy to see the difference between them. This idea of a clear difference or contrast between two things is used in the expression **black and white**.

If you say that something is **black and white**, you mean that the issues involved are very straightforward and it is easy to see what is right and what is wrong. People often use **black and white** to express their disapproval of ideas or ways of thinking which make complicated issues seem more simple than they really are.

*He obviously had no doubt about her business in Havana. It was
all black and white to him.*
The media portray everything in black and white terms.
You might expect him to see everything in black and white.

11.75 Black and white is also used to refer to things that have been
printed rather than said. This is because when things are printed,
they are usually printed in black ink on white paper.

He'd seen the proof in black and white.

grey

11.76 Grey is the colour of ashes or of clouds on a rainy day. Many
people consider **grey** to be a dull and uninteresting colour, and **grey** is
used metaphorically to talk about people or things that are dull or
uninteresting.

...a grey and soulless existence.
...his grey, uninteresting image.

Note that this is spelt **gray** in American English.

*He is little known outside the investment community because he is
modest, gray and unspectacular.*

11.77 Grey is the colour that you get if you mix black and white, and
grey is used metaphorically in a way that is related to the use of **black
and white**, explained at **11.74**, to talk about issues that are not
straightforward or clear because they do not fit easily into a particular category.

If you refer to something as a **grey** area, you mean that people are not
sure how to deal with it, for example because no one is sure who is
responsible for it, or because it does not fit clearly into any particular
category of things.

*One problem is that the description of what in legal terms
constitutes a fixture or a fitting is still a grey area.*
*There are a number of grey areas which a takeover like this
throws up.*

green

11.78 Green is the colour of grass, or of leaves in spring and summer.
Because many plants or parts of plants are green, it is associated with
the earth and things growing on it, and **green** is used metaphorically
to talk about issues which concern the earth, the environment, and
nature.

Green issues are issues which concern saving the environment,
avoiding pollution, and helping to conserve plants and animals.

Green activities and things are activities and things which are designed to achieve these aims.

She is a supporter of green issues.
...green tourism.
These insects also help to control numerous pests without the need for chemicals, an important consideration for the greener gardener.
Cars made of secondhand materials are better and greener.
Thousands of people have turned to the bike as the most economic, greenest and quickest way to travel.

12 Direction and Movement

12.1 A large number of words used to talk about direction and movement are also used metaphorically, especially to talk about the progress that people or plans are making or the way that things are developing. Many of these metaphors are used extremely frequently.

This chapter begins by looking at words for routes to a place, such as **road** and **path**, then looks at words for upward and downward movement, such as **soar**, **climb**, and **plunge**. The last section looks at words associated with ways of moving, such as **gallop** and **stumble**.

Routes

12.2 Many of the words which are used to describe physical journeys are also used to talk about people's lives. Life is referred to as if it were a journey forward, and a person's progress through life is referred to using words such as **route**, **road**, and **path**. Words like these are also used to describe developing processes. These words are usually, but not always, used with positive associations.

route

12.3 A **route** is a way from one place to another. This idea of something that takes you from one place to another is used metaphorically to talk about actions or plans that enable you to achieve a particular thing, and therefore to change the situation you are in.

The **route to** or the **route towards** a particular thing, state, or condition refers to the things people do in order to achieve this thing, state, or condition.

Route is usually used in this way to talk about achieving good things, but it can also be used to talk about getting into bad situations.

> *By the time she was sixteen she had decided that education would be the best route to a good job.*
> *Marriage is not the only route to happiness.*
> *The route towards a market economy would be a very difficult one.*
> *Trying to make employees productive without training them properly is a sure route to disaster.*

road

12.4 A **road** is a long piece of hard ground which is built between two places so that people can drive or ride easily from one place to another. This idea of something that takes you from one place to another is used metaphorically in a similar way to **route** to talk about things that people do in order to achieve a particular thing.

12.5 The **road** to a goal or target is the way in which you hope to achieve that goal or target. For example, if you say that someone is on the **road to** success, or that they are on the **right road**, you mean that they are doing the right things to ensure that they will be successful in the future.

> *They realized that stopping drinking was only the first step on a long and at times difficult <u>road to</u> recovery from alcoholism.*
> *Lets hope he can keep the team on the <u>road to</u> success.*
> *A hundred years ago feminists like Elizabeth Cady Stanton were advocating exercise as the best form of make-up and the <u>right road</u> to beauty.*
> *'I believe,' he said, 'that we are on the right <u>road</u>.'*

12.6 Road can be used to talk about actions or events that have bad results. For example, if you say that someone is on the **road to ruin**, you mean that you think that the thing they are doing or the way they are behaving will have very bad results for them.

> *Fans thought this vicious attack would put her on the <u>road to</u> ruin.*
> *Staff became discontented, the boss was over-worked, team spirit sank to the lowest possible levels and the firm was on the <u>road to</u> disaster.*

12.7 The **road of** a particular change or state is the things that have to be done in order to make that change or achieve that state. For example, **the road of success** is the things that people have to do or achieve in order to be successful. This is a fairly formal use.

Road is often used with this meaning with verbs such as **travel** and **follow**.

> *He must be well aware in private that the people need reassurance if they are to <u>travel</u> along the <u>road of</u> reform.*
> *...<u>following</u> the Soviet Union along the <u>road of</u> economic reform.*

12.8 If you say that someone is on the **road to nowhere**, you think that they are going to fail in what they are doing. If you say that the way someone is behaving is the **road to nowhere**, you think that their behaviour will not achieve anything positive for them.

> *It seems to me that the relationship is on a <u>road to nowhere</u>.*
> *Any rational person must know that violence is a <u>road to nowhere</u>.*
> *Half a century ago, you knew you were on the <u>road to nowhere</u> if you were made minister of education.*

12.9 If you say that a person or something such as an organization or a relationship has reached **the end of the road**, you mean that that person or thing will not achieve anything further or that they are no longer useful.

There is a growing feeling that the NLD may have reached the
end of its current political road.

12.10 Note that the plural form **roads** is not usually used metaphorically.

avenue

12.11 An **avenue** is a wide, straight road, often with trees on either
side. **Avenue** is used metaphorically in a similar way to **road** and
route to talk about plans, actions, or opportunities that enable
someone to achieve something or to change the situation they are in.

If you say that you are going to explore a particular **avenue** in order to
achieve something, you mean that you are going to find out about a
certain plan or opportunity to see if it can help you to achieve that
thing. If you say that something is an **avenue** for change, you mean
that it is an opportunity or a way of behaving that will allow you to
change.

This use of **avenue** is more formal than the metaphorical uses of
route and **road**, and is usually used in written English, especially
journalism.

She has explored all the available avenues for change.
Alison made it clear that she was eager to pursue other avenues.
Another avenue of research is to look at other plants.

path

12.12 A **path** is a strip of ground which people walk on, and which
leads from one place to another. Like **road**, **route**, and **avenue**, **path**
is used to talk about things that people do and the results that these
things have. **Path** is used especially to talk about choices that people
make.

12.13 You can refer to the way that someone chooses to lead their life,
and to their choices in their professional and personal life as their
path in life, especially when you want to talk about the way that they
achieve a particular thing. For example, if you are deciding which
path to take after you leave school, you are deciding what you want to
do when you leave school and thinking about the things you will have
to do in order to achieve this; a person's **career path** is the way their
career is progressing and the things that they will have to do in order
to reach a particular level or have a particular status. This use is most
common in written English.

Path is often used in this way with verbs such as **take** and **follow**.

This can prevent you from seeing which path to take in your
career.
A very long time ago, I decided on a change of career path—I was
going to be a flight steward.

His father offered to give Alex £200 a month so that he could follow his chosen path of becoming an artist.

12.14 You can refer to the choices that people or groups of people make, or to the things that they choose to do in order to reach a particular situation, state, or condition, as a particular **path**. This use is most common in written English, especially journalism.

...the right of every nation to choose its own path of social development.
...countries which have already moved further than others along the path of social progress.
The President said his country would continue on its path to full democracy.
This job isn't a path to riches.

step

12.15 If you take a **step**, you lift one foot and put it down in another place, for example, when you are walking. This idea of moving in a particular direction is used metaphorically to talk about an action which will help someone to achieve a particular goal, especially when that action is one of a number of actions that they will have to take.

For example, if you take the first **step** towards becoming a teacher, you do the first thing that is necessary if you want to become a teacher, such as studying at a particular college.

Step is often used in this way with words such as **road** and **path**.

Scientists have taken a big step in understanding Alzheimer's disease.
The setting-up of stock-exchanges is an important step on the road to a free-market economy.
If you feel that you have reason to be worried, the first step is to make an appointment to see your family doctor.
Many salespeople have the mistaken belief that making a sale is the last step in the selling process.

Here are some examples of words commonly used before **step** in this way:

backward	giant	short
big	great	significant
critical	important	small
decisive	major	third
each	new	unprecedented
every	next	unusual
first	positive	
further	second	

12.16 If you do something **step by step**, you do it carefully, thinking about each stage before you move on to the next. A **step-by-step**

approach to something is one in which you consider each stage
carefully. A **step-by-step** guide to doing something is a guide
designed to help beginners by explaining each stage very carefully.

> *It was a gradual process which could only be carried out step by
> step.*
> *The book is full of facts, advice and step-by-step guides; it's just
> like having an expert at your side.*

12.17 If two or more people who are walking or dancing together are
in step, they are moving their feet forward at exactly the same time as
each other; if two or more people who are walking or dancing together
are **out of step**, their feet are moving forward at different times, often
with the result that their walking or dancing looks awkward and
clumsy. **In step** and **out of step** are used metaphorically to talk about
whether or not people's ideas or opinions are similar and work
together well.

If one person is **in step** with another, their ideas or opinions are
similar and they work well together.

If one person is **out of step** with another, their ideas or opinions are
different, with the result that they do not work well together and often
disagree about things.

> *Moscow is anxious to stay in step with Washington.*
> *They have found themselves out of step with the Prime Minister
> on this issue.*

fast lane, slow lane

12.18 On busy roads such as motorways in Britain or freeways in the
United States, the traffic is divided into lanes, with one of the lanes for
traffic that is moving very quickly, sometimes called **the fast lane**,
and one for traffic that is moving quite slowly, sometimes called **the
slow lane**. **Fast lane** and **slow lane** are used metaphorically to talk
about the kind of life someone has and how busy or exciting it seems to
be.

12.19 You can say that someone is in **the fast lane** if they are very
busy and do a lot of exciting things, such as meeting famous people or
travelling abroad. You can refer to this kind of life as **life in the fast
lane**.

When **fast lane** is used in this way, it usually has positive associations.

> *Cooper moved quickly into the fast lane of Hollywood society.*
> *He is still adapting to life in the fast lane.*

12.20 You can say that someone is in **the slow lane** if they do not do many exciting or stressful things. You can refer to this kind of life as **life in the slow lane**.

Slow lane can be used in this way with both negative and positive associations.

> *Rather than moving over into the slow lane he has been having fun proving his critics wrong.*
> *...seven days of good food, fine wine, and living in the slow lane.*
> *At the moment, for us, it's life in the slow lane, whether we like it or not.*

superhighway

12.21 In American English, a **superhighway** is a large road with eight lanes which allows a large number of vehicles to travel very quickly. This idea of something that allows lots of things to move quickly is used metaphorically to talk about the way large amounts of information can be quickly exchanged by computers.

The information **superhighway** is the network of computer links that enables computer users all over the world to communicate with each other quickly and efficiently.

> *Many cable TV and telephone firms prefer to collaborate, rather than compete, in building America's information superhighway.*
> *The construction of a superhighway of knowledge will have as profound an impact on the American economy as the development of the national railroad system in the 1800s.*

Movement upwards and downwards

12.22 A large number of words, especially verbs, which are used to talk about movement upwards and downwards are also used metaphorically. The main metaphorical uses are most common in journalism, especially to talk about economics and the stock market.

These words are also used to talk about people's feelings. If you use a word describing upward movement to describe your feelings, you mean that you are feeling happier; words for downward movements are used to describe feelings of unhappiness.

This section begins with words used to talk about upward movement, such as **soar** and **climb**, then it looks at words used to talk about downward movement, such as **plunge** and **plummet**.

soar

12.23 If something such as a bird **soars** into the air, it moves quickly up into the air. This idea of moving upwards very quickly is used to talk about amounts or levels which increase quickly.

12.24 If the volume, level, or amount of something **soars**, it increases very quickly and in a way that seems to be out of control. This use is most common in journalism, especially to talk about things related to the economy such as prices, inflation, or unemployment.

Unemployment has soared and inflation has been running at more than 20% a month.
The problem is that food prices have soared in the north.
The price of a pint of beer is soaring in Britain's pubs.
Sales of mobile phones are set to soar by more than a million over the next year.

12.25 If your spirits **soar**, you suddenly feel very happy. This is a literary use.

When a sale was made Marianne was happy for him. His spirits would briefly soar. But afterwards depression would set in.
For the first time in months, my spirits soared.

climb

12.26 If you **climb** something such as a tree, mountain, or ladder, or if you **climb up** it, you move towards the top of it. **Climb** is used metaphorically in a similar way to **soar**, to talk about amounts or levels increasing.

12.27 If something **climbs**, it increases steadily in value or amount.

The shares climbed 2p to 26p.
By the early 1980s, 2% of the population were vegetarian. In 1991 the figure has climbed to 7%.
The market then settled down and share prices began to climb sharply again.

12.28 Journalists sometimes refer to the gradual increase of an amount as a **climb** in that amount. Journalists also sometimes refer to a slow, steady improvement in a bad situation such as a recession as a **climb out** of that situation.

...a climb in the price of precious metals.
...as we begin the long slow climb out of the recession.

plunge

12.29 If someone or something **plunges** in a particular direction, they move quickly downwards in that direction, usually because they have fallen, jumped, or been pushed in that direction. This idea of moving quickly downwards is used metaphorically to talk about levels or amounts which decrease very quickly. It is also used to talk about someone suddenly finding themself in a particular situation.

12.30 If the price, volume, or amount of something **plunges**, it decreases very quickly and in a way that seems to be out of control. This use is most common in journalism, especially to talk about things related to the economy, such as prices, inflation, or unemployment.

Plunge is usually used in this way to suggest that the sudden decrease is a bad thing.

Profits plunged and he stood down as chairman last January.
The bank's profits had plunged by 80%.
The price of gold plunged 7% in a single day.
Analysts worry about the plunging value of these companies.

12.31 If someone **plunges** or **is plunged** into a bad situation, they are forced into that situation and find it difficult to change or improve things.

Inner-cities have plunged deeper into despair.
The twenty-five pound fine plunged him into a world of petty crime and unemployment.
...events which plunged the whole country into a bitter and destructive civil war.

12.32 If you **plunge into** an activity, you suddenly get very involved in it.

Feeling much better, he plunged headlong into work.
Eleanor returned to Washington and plunged into her new life.
He starts the day with American television interviews and then plunges into a series of meetings.

plummet

12.33 If someone or something **plummets**, they fall very quickly. **Plummet** is used metaphorically in a similar way to **plunge**, to talk about levels or amounts decreasing very quickly. It is also used to talk about people suddenly becoming unhappy or unpopular.

12.34 If the level or amount of something **plummets**, it decreases suddenly and in a way that seems to be out of control. This use is most common in journalism, especially to talk about things related to the economy, such as prices, inflation, or unemployment.

Plummet is usually used in this way to suggest that the sudden decrease is a bad thing.

> *With the collapse of the economy, all the big buyers vanished and prices plummeted.*
> *Opinion polls indicate that its support has plummeted to around 5%.*
> *...the plummeting price of computers.*

12.35 If your confidence **plummets**, you suddenly begin to feel much less confident than you were. If your popularity **plummets**, you suddenly become much less popular than you were.

> *Your self-esteem can plummet at just a word.*
> *As the months have gone by and he has largely failed to deal with the country's pressing economic and social problems, his popularity has plummeted.*

12.36 If your spirits **plummet**, you suddenly feel very unhappy.

> *It wasn't so much the ageing process itself that sent my spirits plummeting although greying hair and wrinkles weren't exactly adding to my self-esteem.*

slump

12.37 If you **slump** somewhere, you fall or sit down there very quickly or suddenly, for example, because you are ill or very tired. **Slump** is used metaphorically in a similar way to **plummet** and **plunge** to talk about levels or amounts which fall quickly.

12.38 If the level, amount, or value of something **slumps**, it falls, usually because people are no longer interested in it or because there is less demand for it. This use is most common in journalism.

> *Demand for fur coats has slumped under pressure from animal rights organizations.*
> *For the past three years, the company's advertising revenues have slumped.*
> *Union membership has slumped, as a proportion of the workforce, to its lowest since the 1920s.*

12.39 If a particular business or market is in a **slump**, there is less buying and selling than usual, so people are making less profit than previously. If a country is **in a slump**, its economy has slowed down greatly and there is more unemployment and poverty than usual.

> *The luxury car maker is putting 4,000 employees on a shorter working week because of a slump in sales.*
> *This will lead to a further slump in the housing market.*
> *These figures indicate a slump in one of the world's most successful economies.*

MPs have voted themselves another pay increase. Have they forgotten we are <u>in a slump</u>?

tumble

12.40 If someone or something **tumbles** somewhere, they fall there with a rolling, bouncing movement. Like **plunge** and **plummet**, **tumble** is used metaphorically to talk about levels or amounts decreasing quickly.

Note that this use of **tumble** is less common than the metaphorical uses of **plunge** and **plummet**.

If a level, amount, or price **tumbles**, it falls suddenly and unexpectedly. This use is most common in journalism.

The annual rate of inflation <u>tumbled</u> to 2.6% in December, the lowest level in six years.
Financial markets <u>are tumbling</u> as worries about the economy increase.
Prices <u>have tumbled</u> by up to 40% in some areas.

12.41 You can also say that something such as an amount or value **takes a tumble** if it falls suddenly. This use is most common in journalism.

...if the pound <u>takes a tumble</u> on the foreign exchange markets.
Shares <u>took a</u> serious <u>tumble</u> yesterday.

dip

12.42 If something **dips**, it makes a downward movement, usually quite quickly. **Dip** is used metaphorically in a similar way to **plunge** and **plummet**, to talk about levels or amounts decreasing, but unlike **plunge** and **plummet**, **dip** is used to suggest that the level or amount may rise again soon.

If something such as a price or an amount **dips**, it drops below its usual level, often for only a short time. This use is most common in journalism.

Prices <u>have dipped</u> slightly in recent weeks.
The economy will become even more excitable and the markets <u>may dip</u>.
The unemployment rate <u>dipped</u> to 7.4% in October.

12.43 A **dip** in the level or amount of something is a slight decrease in it, often one which is only expected to last for a short time. This use is most common in journalism.

Opinion polls show a huge <u>dip</u> in enthusiasm for the monarchy.
...a profits <u>dip</u>.

Ways of moving

12.44 A number of words used to talk about ways of moving are also used metaphorically to talk about things which are related to economics, such as prices, and to talk about companies and governments and whether or not they are successful. They are also sometimes used to talk about people's lives and how they are progressing.

gallop

12.45 When a horse **gallops**, it moves very fast, so that all four legs are off the ground at the same time in each stride. This idea of something moving forwards very quickly is used metaphorically to talk about levels or amounts which increase quickly, or organizations which seem to be developing very quickly.

If something such as a system or process **gallops**, it develops very quickly, often in a way that is difficult to control. This use is most common in journalism.

> *That is very low by the standards of the mid 1980s, when China's economy galloped ahead.*
> *The galloping inflation of the previous two years seemed to have been brought under control.*
> *...galloping price rises.*

runaway

12.46 A **runaway** vehicle or animal is moving forwards very quickly, and its driver or rider has lost control of it. **Runaway** is used metaphorically to describe things such as systems or price increases that seem to be developing in a way that no one can control. For example, **runaway** inflation is at a very high level, and no one seems to be able to do anything to bring it down or to stop it increasing more; if a product is a **runaway** seller, it is selling much more quickly than people expected it to. This use is most common in journalism.

> *In just six months, the country's runaway inflation has been brought under control.*
> *...an economy in crisis and runaway public spending.*
> *Hawking's 'A Brief History of Time' was a runaway bestseller, a book that sold millions.*

stagger

12.47 If someone **staggers**, they walk very unsteadily, for example because they are ill or drunk. This idea of moving unsteadily in a way that suggests illness or weakness is used metaphorically to talk about organizations or systems that seem to have a lot of problems and do not seem to be working very well.

If something such as an organization or system **staggers**, it seems to have a lot of problems so it is not working very well, and may seem to be about to fail completely. This use is most common in journalism.

> *The Service will continue to stagger from crisis to crisis.*
> *The marriage staggered on for a little while longer.*

lurch

12.48 To **lurch** means to make a sudden, unintentional, jerky movement, usually forwards. This idea of movements or actions which are not intentional is used metaphorically to talk about people or organizations which seem to be having a lot of problems.

If something such as a government or economy **lurches** from one bad condition or state to another, it is functioning badly and constantly having problems, and no one appears to have any control over its progress. This use is most common in journalism.

> *The state government has lurched from one budget crisis to another.*
> *The economy, meanwhile, lurches from bad to worse.*

12.49 You can also use **lurch** as a noun to refer to a change which no one seems to have planned or foreseen.

> *This marks a new and dangerous lurch in foreign policy.*
> *These sales are part of a lurch from communism towards capitalism.*

stumble

12.50 If you **stumble**, you put your foot down awkwardly when you are walking or running and nearly fall over. **Stumble** is used metaphorically to talk about systems or organizations which seem to be having a lot of problems.

12.51 If you say that a person, company, or government **is stumbling along**, you mean that they are doing their job, but with frequent problems. If you say that they **stumble**, you mean that they make a serious mistake and nearly fail completely. You can also say that a person, company, or government **stumbles from** one bad situation **to** another when they have frequent serious problems.

> *That is why western politicians have stumbled along with their present policy of aid and peacekeeping.*
> *The company stumbled in the late 1980s when it rushed a new machine to market and allowed costs to soar.*

He had a depressing three years, during which he <u>stumbled from</u> one crisis <u>to</u> another.
Britain, for instance, had a <u>stumbling</u> economy and a government under pressure.

12.52 Stumble is also used in the phrasal verbs **stumble across** and **stumble upon** to talk about things that seem to happen by accident.

If someone **stumbles across** or **stumbles on** something useful or important, they find it, when they were not looking for it.

Many important scientific discoveries <u>have been stumbled across</u> by accident.
The customs men were obviously hoping that they <u>had stumbled on</u> a major drug-trafficking ring.

slide

12.53 If something **slides** somewhere, or if you **slide** it there, it moves there smoothly over or against something else. **Slide** is used metaphorically to talk about situations that seem to be gradually getting worse in a way that no one can control.

12.54 If something **is sliding**, it seems to be gradually getting worse or decreasing in amount, in a way that cannot be controlled.

As a man, he remains popular, but his political ratings <u>are sliding</u>.
New York's residential property prices <u>have been sliding</u> since 1988.

12.55 If someone **is sliding** into an undesirable situation, they seem to be moving into that situation in a way that they cannot control.

Decisive steps had to be taken to stop the country <u>sliding</u> into disaster.
The province is quite close to <u>sliding</u> into civil war.
...youngsters in danger of <u>sliding</u> into crime.

12.56 You can also use **slide** as a noun to refer to a state or condition which is gradually getting worse, in a way that will be difficult to reverse later.

...failing to stop the <u>slide</u> in the company's fortunes.
There may be depression or a slippery <u>slide</u> into alcoholism.

Index

Items in roman are words that are discussed in chapters 1–12. Items in *italic* are ideas, people, or books that are discussed in the **Introduction**. Numbers refer to the chapter and section, except where it is stated otherwise.

a shadow of your former self 11.49
sharpen 5.58–5.62
shed 8.82–8.84, 11.11
   shed light 11.11
sheep 3.54
sheepish 3.55
shine 11.32
shoot 8.20
   green shoots of recovery 8.20
shoulder 1.1, 1.32, 1.33
shower 9.25–9.27
   shower with 9.27
shrew 3.72
shrewish 3.73
shrivel 8.1, 8.81
shut
   shut the door on something 4.50, 4.51
sick 2.15–2.18, 2.19
sickness 1.60, 2.19
side
   on the bright side 11.20
   dark side 11.36
silence
   wall of silence 4.39
simmer 7.23, 7.38–7.40, 10.77
   simmer down 7.40
skate 6.44–6.46
   skate around 6.44, 6.45
   skate on thin ice 6.46
   skate over 6.44, 6.45
skeleton 1.1, 1.84
   skeleton staff 1.84
slam
   slam the door on something 4.50, 4.51
slice 7.10–7.15
   a slice of life 7.14
   a slice of the action 7.15
slide 12.53–12.56
slog
   slog your guts out 1.66
slow
   slow lane 12.18, 12.20
slump 12.37–12.39
smoulder 10.73–10.76
snow 9.9
   snowed under 9.9
soar 12.1, 12.22–12.25, 12.26
social animal 3.5
sour 7.70–7.74

go sour 7.72, 7.73
turn sour 7.73
sourly 7.75
sourness 7.76
sow 8.52–8.54
   sow the seeds of something 8.54
spark 10.69–10.72
   spark off 10.72
spice 7.48, 7.49
spicy 7.50, 7.56
spine 1.1, 1.88
spineless 1.88
sport 6.32–6.35
   bad sport 6.35
   good sport 6.33, 6.34
sporting chance 6.37
sprout 8.74
squirrel 3.77
   squirrel away 3.77
staff
   skeleton staff 1.84
stagger 12.47
stake 6.74–6.77
   at stake 6.75
stakes 6.78
   the stakes are high 6.76
stalemate 6.19
steer 5.78–5.82
   steer away from something 5.80
   steer clear of something 5.82
stem 8.21
step 5.72, 12.15–12.17
   in step 12.17
   out of step 12.17
   step up a gear 5.72
step by step 12.16
step-by-step 12.16
stew 7.27–7.31
   stew in your own juice 7.28
stomach 1.60–1.62
   cannot stomach something 1.61
   to not have the stomach for something 1.62
storm 9.47–9.54, 9.55, 9.62
   a storm breaks 9.48
   a storm is gathering 9.48
   go down a storm 9.51
   take someone or something by storm 9.50
   weather a storm 9.48
stormy 9.55